KT-512-074

Praise for the Montalbano series

'The novels of Andrea Camilleri breathe out
the sense of place, the sense of humour, and the sense
of despair that fill the air of Sicily. To read him is
to be taken to that glorious, tortured island'
Donna Leon

'Andrea Camilleri's novels set in Sicily, and translated by the
poet Stephen Sartarelli, are among the most exquisitely
crafted pieces of crime writing available today. *The Patience of
the Spider* is no exception; a plot based around the mysterious
kidnapping of a student is simply superb'
Sunday Times

'Both farcical and endearing, Montalbano is a cross between
Columbo and Chandler's Philip Marlowe, with the added
culinary idiosyncrasies of an Italian Maigret . . . The smells,
colours and landscapes of Sicily come to life'
Guardian

'Sly and witty . . . Montalbano must pick his way through a
labyrinth of corruption, false clues, vendettas – and delicious
meals. The result is funny and intriguing with a fluent
translation by New York poet Stephen Sartarelli'
Observer

'Delightful . . . funny and ebulliently atmospheric'
The Times

'This savagely funny police procedural proves that
sardonic laughter is a sound that translates ever so smoothly
into English'
New York Times Book Review

THE SNACK THIEF

Andrea Camilleri is one of Italy's most famous
contemporary writers. His Montalbano series has been
adapted for Italian television and translated
into nine languages. He lives in Rome.

Stephen Sartarelli is an award-winning translator.
He is also the author of three books of poetry, most
recently *The Open Vault*. He lives in France.

ANDREA CAMILLERI

THE SNACK THIEF

Translated by Stephen Sartarelli

PICADOR

First published 2003 by Viking Penguin,
a member of Penguin Putnam Inc., New York

First published in Great Britain 2004 by Picador

First published in paperback 2005 by Picador
an imprint of Pan Macmillan, a division of Macmillan Publishers Limited
Pan Macmillan, 20 New Wharf Road, London N1 9RR
Basingstoke and Oxford
Associated companies throughout the world
www.panmacmillan.com

ISBN 978-0-330-49297-3

12 14 16 18 19 17 15 13 11

A CIP catalogue record for this book is available from
the British Library.

Typeset by Intype Libra Ltd
Printed and bound in the UK by
CPI Mackays, Chatham ME5 8TD

Visit **www.picador.com** to read more about all our books and to buy
them. You will also find features, author interviews and news of any author
events, and you can sign up for e-newsletters so that you're always first to hear
about our new releases.

THE SNACK THIEF

ONE

He woke up in a bad way. The sheets, during the sweaty, restless sleep that had followed his wolfing down three pounds of sardines *a beccafico* the previous evening, had wound themselves tightly round his body, making him feel like a mummy. He got up, went into the kitchen, opened the refrigerator, and guzzled half a bottle of cold water. As he was drinking, he glanced out of the wide-open window. The dawn light promised a good day. The sea was as flat as a table, the sky clear and cloudless. Sensitive as he was to the weather, Montalbano felt reassured as to his mood in the hours to come. Because it was still too early to get up, he went back to bed and readied himself for two more hours of slumber, pulling the sheet over his head. He thought, as he always did before falling asleep, of Livia lying in her bed in Boccadasse, outside Genoa. She was a soothing presence, propitious to any journey, long or short, 'in country sleep', as Dylan Thomas had put it in a poem he liked very much.

No sooner had the journey begun when it was inter-rupted by the ringing of the telephone. Like a drill, the sound seemed to enter one ear and come out of the other, boring through his brain.

'Hello!'

'Whoozis I'm speaking with?'

'Tell me first who you are.'

'This is Catarella.'

'What's the matter?'

'Sorry, Chief, I din't rec'nize your voice as yours. You mighta been sleeping.'

'I certainly might have, at five in the morning! Would you please tell me what the hell is the matter without busting my balls any further?'

'Somebody was killed in Mazàra del Vallo.'

'What the fuck is that to me? I'm in Vigàta.'

'But, Chief, the dead guy—'

Montalbano hung up and unplugged the phone. Before shutting his eyes he thought that perhaps his friend Valente, vice-commissioner of Mazàra, was looking for him. He would call him later, from his office.

*

The shutter slammed hard against the wall. Montalbano sat bolt upright in bed, eyes agape with fright, convinced, in the haze of sleep still enveloping him, that he'd been shot at. In the twinkling of an eye, the weather had changed: a cold, humid wind was kicking up waves with a yellowish froth, the sky was now entirely covered with clouds that threatened rain.

Cursing the saints, he got up, went into the bathroom, turned on the shower and lathered himself. All at once the water ran out. In Vigàta, and therefore also in Marinella, where he lived, water was distributed roughly every three days. Roughly, because there was no way of knowing whether you would have water the very next day or the following week. For this reason Montalbano had taken the precaution of having several large tanks installed on the roof of his house, which would fill up when water was available. This time, however, there had apparently been no new water for eight days, for that was the maximum autonomy granted him by his reserves. He ran into the kitchen, put a pot under the tap to collect the meagre trickle that came out, and did the same in the bathroom sink. With the bit of water thus collected, he somehow managed to rinse the soap off his body, but the whole procedure certainly didn't help his mood.

While driving to Vigàta, yelling obscenities at all the motorists to cross his path – whose only use for the Highway Code, in his opinion, was to wipe their arses with it, one way or another – he remembered Catarella's phone call and the explanation he'd come up with for it, which didn't make sense. If Valente had needed him for some homicide that took place in Mazàra, he would have called him at home, not at headquarters. He had concocted that explanation for convenience's sake, to unburden his conscience and sleep for another two hours in peace.

*

'There's absolutely nobody here!' Catarella told him as soon as he saw him, respectfully rising from his chair at the switchboard. Montalbano had decided, with Sergeant Fazio's agreement, that this was the best place for him. Even with his habit of passing on the wildest, most unlikely phone calls, he would surely do less damage there than anywhere else.

'What is it, a holiday?'

'No, Chief, it's not a holiday. They're all down at the port because of that dead guy in Mazàra I called you about, if you remember, sometime early this morning or thereabouts.'

'But if the dead guy's in Mazàra, what are they all doing at the port?'

'No, Chief, the dead guy's here.'

'But, Jesus Christ, if the dead guy's here, why the hell are you telling me he's in Mazàra?'

'Because he was from Mazàra. That's where he worked.'

'Cat, think for a minute, so to speak . . . or whatever it is that you do: if a tourist from Bergamo was killed here in Vigàta, what would you tell me? That somebody was killed in Bergamo?'

'Chief, the point is, this dead guy was just passing through. I mean, they shot him when he was on a fishing boat from Mazàra.'

'Who shot him?'

'The Tunisians did, Chief.'

Montalbano gave up, demoralized.

'Did Augello also go down to the port?'

'Yessir.'

His second-in-command, Mimì Augello, would be delighted if he didn't show up at the port.

'Listen, Cat I have to write a report. I'm not in for anyone.'

*

'Hello, Chief? I got Signorina Livia on the line here from Genoa. What do I do, Chief? Should I put her on or not?'

'Put her on.'

'Since you said, not ten minutes ago, that you wasn't in for nobody—'

'I said put her on, Cat . . . Hello, Livia? Hi.'

'Hi, my eye. I've been trying to call you all morning. The phone at your house just rings and rings.'

'Really? I suppose I forgot to plug it back in. You want to hear something funny? At five o'clock this morning, I got a phone call about—'

'I don't want to hear anything funny. I tried ringing at seven-thirty, at eight-fifteen, I tried again at—'

'Livia, I already told you I forgot—'

'You forgot *me*, that's what you forgot. I told you yesterday I was going to phone you at seven-thirty this morning to decide whether—'

'Livia, I'm warning you. It's windy outside and about to rain.'

'So what?'

'You know what. This kind of weather puts me in a bad mood. I wouldn't want my words to be—'

1

'I get the picture. I just won't phone you any more. You phone me, if you feel like it.'

∗

'Montalbano! How are you? Officer Augello told me everything. This is a very big deal, one that will certainly have international repercussions. Don't you think?'

Montalbano felt at sea. He had no idea what the commissioner was talking about. He decided to be generically affirmative.

'Oh, yes, yes.'

International repercussions?

'Anyway, I've arranged for Augello to confer with the prefect. The matter is, how shall I say, beyond my competence.'

'Yes, yes.'

'Are you feeling all right, Montalbano?'

'Yes, fine. Why?'

'Nothing, it just seemed . . .'

'Just a slight headache, that's all.'

'What day is today?'

'Thursday, sir.'

'Listen, why don't you come to dinner at our house on Saturday? My wife'll make you her black spaghetti in squid ink. It's delicious.'

Pasta with squid ink. His mood was black enough to dress a hundred pounds of spaghetti. International repercussions?

∗

Fazio came in and Montalbano immediately laid into him.

'Would somebody please be so kind as to tell me what the fuck is going on?'

'C'mon, Chief, don't take it out on me just because it's windy outside. For my part, early this morning, before contacting Inspector Augello, I had somebody phone you.'

'You mean Catarella? If you have Catarella phoning me about something important, then you really must be a shit-head, since you know damn well that nobody can ever understand a fucking thing the guy says. What happened, anyway?'

'A motor trawler from Mazàra, which according to the ship's captain was fishing in international waters, was attacked by a Tunisian patrol boat and sprayed with machine-gun fire. The fishing boat signalled its position to one of our patrols, the *Fulmine*, then managed to escape.'

'Good going,' said Montalbano.

'On whose part?' asked Fazio.

'On the part of the captain of the fishing boat, who instead of surrendering had the courage to run away. What else?'

'The shots killed one of the crew.'

'Somebody from Mazàra?'

'Sort of.'

'Would you please explain?'

'He was Tunisian. They say his working papers were in order. Down around Mazàra all the crews are mixed. First of all because they're good workers, and secondly because, if they're ever stopped, they can talk to the patrols from the other side.'

'Do you believe the trawler was fishing in international waters?'

'Me? Do I look like a moron or something?'

✻

'Hello, Inspector Montalbano? This is Major Marniti of the Harbour Office.'

'What can I do for you, Major?'

'I'm calling about that unfortunate incident on the Mazarese fishing boat, where the Tunisian was killed. I'm questioning the captain, trying to determine exactly where they were at the moment they were attacked, and to establish the sequence of events. Afterwards, he's going to drop into your office.'

'Why? Hasn't my assistant already questioned him?'

'Yes.'

'Then there's really no need for him to come here. Thanks for calling.'

They were trying to drag him into this mess by the ear.

✻

The door flew open with such force that the inspector jumped out of his chair. Catarella appeared, looking very agitated.

'Sorry 'bout that, Chief. Door slipped outa my hand.'

'If you ever come in like that again, I'll shoot you. What is it?'

'Somebody just now phoned that somebody's inside a lift.'

The inkwell, made of finely wrought bronze, missed Catarella's forehead but made such a noise when it struck the wooden door that it could have been a cannon shot. Catarella cringed, covering his head with his arms. Montalbano started kicking his desk. In rushed Fazio, his hand on his open holster.

'What was that? What happened?'

'Get this arsehole to explain to you this business about somebody stuck in a lift. Let 'em call the damn fire department! But get him out of here, I don't want to hear his voice.'

Fazio returned in a flash.

'Somebody got killed in a lift,' he said, brief and to the point, to pre-empt any further flying inkwells.

*

'Giuseppe Cosentino, security guard,' said the man standing near the open lift door, introducing himself. 'I was the one who found Mr Lapècora.'

'How come there's nobody around? Where are all the nosy neighbours?' Fazio asked in amazement.

'I sent them all home. They do what I say around here. I live on the sixth floor,' the security guard said proudly, adjusting the jacket of his uniform.

Montalbano wondered how much authority Giuseppe Cosentino would have if he lived in the basement.

The dead Mr Lapècora was sitting on the floor of the

lift, with his shoulders propped against the rear wall. Next to his right hand was a bottle of Corvo white, still corked and sealed. Next to his left hand, a light grey hat. Dressed to the nines, tie and all, the late Mr Lapècora was a distinguished-looking man of about sixty, with eyes open in a look of astonishment, perhaps for having wet his trousers. Montalbano bent down and with the tip of his forefinger touched the dark stain between the dead man's legs. It wasn't piss, but blood. The lift was one of those set inside the wall, so there was no way to look behind the corpse to see if the man had been stabbed or shot. He took a deep breath and didn't smell any gunpowder, though it was possible it had already dissipated.

They needed to alert the coroner.

'You think Dr Pasquano is still at the port or would he already be back in Montelusa by now?'

'Probably still at the port.'

'Go and give him a ring. And if Jacomuzzi and the forensics gang are there, tell them to come too.'

Fazio raced out. Montalbano turned to the security guard, who, sensing he was about to be addressed, came to attention.

'At ease,' Montalbano said wearily.

The inspector learned that the building had six floors, with three apartments per floor, all inhabited.

'I live on the sixth floor, the top floor,' Giuseppe Cosentino felt compelled to reaffirm.

'Was Mr Lapècora married?'

'Yessir. To Antonietta Palmisano.'

'Did you send the widow home too?'

'No sir. She doesn't know she's a widow yet, sir. She went out early this morning to visit her sister in Fiacca, seeing as how this sister's not in good health. She took the six-thirty bus.'

'Excuse me, but how do you know all these things?'

Did living on the sixth floor grant him that power too? Did they all have to tell him what they were doing and why?

'Mrs Palmisano Lapècora told my wife yesterday,' the security guard explained. 'Seeing as how the two women talk to each other and everything.'

'Do the Lapècoras have any children?'

'One son. He's a doctor. But he lives a long way from Vigàta.'

'What was Lapècora's profession?'

'Businessman. Had his office in Salita Granet, number twenty-eight. But in the last few years, he only went there three times a week: Monday, Wednesday and Friday, seeing as how he didn't feel much like working any more. He had some money stashed away, didn't have to depend on anyone.'

'You are a gold mine, Mr Cosentino.'

The security guard sprang back to attention.

At that moment, a woman of about fifty appeared, with legs like tree trunks. Her hands were loaded with plastic bags filled to bursting.

'I went shopping!' she declared with a surly glance at the inspector and the security guard.

'I'm glad,' said Montalbano.

'Well I'm not, all right? Because now I have to climb up six flights of stairs. When are you going to take the body away?'

And, glaring again at the two men, she began her difficult ascent, snorting like an enraged bull.

'A terrible woman, Mr Inspector. Her name is Gaetana Pinna. She lives in the apartment next to mine, and not a day goes by without her trying to start an argument with my wife, who, since she's a real lady, won't give her the satisfaction. And so the woman gets even by making a horrible racket, especially when I'm trying to catch up on my sleep after my long shift.'

*

The handle of the knife stuck between Mr Lapècora's shoulder blades was worn. A common kitchen utensil.

'When did they kill him, in your opinion?' the inspector asked Dr Pasquano.

'To make a rough guess, I'd say between seven and eight o'clock this morning. I'll be able to tell you more precisely a little later.'

Jacomuzzi arrived with his men from the crime lab, and they began their intricate search.

Montalbano stepped out of the building's main door. It was windy, the sky still overcast. The street was a very short one, with only two shops, one opposite the other. On the left-hand side of the street was a greengrocer, behind whose counter sat a very thin man with thick glasses. One of the lenses was cracked.

'Hello, I'm Inspector Montalbano. This morning, did you by any chance see Mr Lapècora come in or go out of the front door of his building?'

The thin man chuckled and said nothing.

'Did you hear my question?' asked the inspector, slightly miffed.

'Oh, I heard you all right,' the greengrocer said. 'But as for seeing, I can't help you much there. I couldn't even see a tank if one came through that door.'

On the right-hand side of the street was a fishmonger's shop, with two customers inside. The inspector waited for them to come out, then entered.

'Hello, Lollo.'

'Hello, Inspector. I've got some really fresh striped bream today.'

'I'm not here to buy fish, Lollo.'

'You're here about the death.'

'Yeah.'

'How'd Lapècora die?'

'A knife in the back.'

Lollo looked at him open mouthed.

'Lapècora was murdered?!'

'Why so surprised?'

'Who would have wished Mr Lapècora any harm? He was a good man, Mr Lapècora. Unbelievable!'

'Did you see him this morning?'

'No.'

'What time did you open up?'

ANDREA CAMILLERI

'Six-thirty. Ah, but I did run into his wife, Antonietta, on the corner. She was in a rush.'

'She was running to catch the bus for Fiacca.'

In all likelihood, Montalbano concluded, Lapècora was killed in the lift, as he was about to go out. He lived on the fourth floor.

*

Dr Pasquano took the body to Montelusa for the autopsy. Meanwhile, Jacomuzzi wasted a little more time filling three small plastic bags with a cigarette butt, a bit of dust and a tiny piece of wood.

'I'll keep you posted.'

Montalbano went into the lift and signalled to the security guard, who had not moved an inch all the while, to come along with him. Cosentino seemed hesitant.

'What's wrong?'

'There's still blood on the floor.'

'So what? Just be careful not to get it on your shoes. Would you rather climb six flights of stairs?'

TWO

'Come in, come in,' said a cheerful Signora Cosentino, an irresistibly likeable balloon with a moustache.

Montalbano entered a living room with the dining room attached. The housewife turned to her husband with a look of concern.

'You weren't able to rest, Pepè.'

'Duty. And when duty calls, duty calls.'

'Did you go out this morning, signora?'

'I never go out before Pepè comes home.'

'Do you know Mrs Lapècora?'

'Yes. We chat a little, now and then, when we're waiting for the lift together.'

'Did you also chat with the husband?'

'No, I didn't care much for him. A good man, no doubt about that, but I just didn't like him. If you'll excuse me a minute . . .'

She left the room. Montalbano turned to the security guard.

'Where do you work?'

'At the salt depot. From eight in the evening to eight in the morning.'

'It was you who discovered the body, correct?'

'Yes, sir. It must've been about ten past eight at the latest. The depot's just around the corner. I called the lift—'

'It wasn't on the ground floor?'

'No, it wasn't. I distinctly remember calling it.'

'And of course you don't know what floor it was on.'

'I've thought about that, Inspector. Based on the amount of time it took to arrive, I'd say it was on the fifth floor. I think I calculated right.'

It didn't add up. All decked out, Mr Lapècora . . .

'What was his first name, by the way?'

'Aurelio, but he went by Arelio.'

. . . instead of taking the lift down, took it up one floor. The grey hat meant he was about to go outside, not to visit someone inside the building.

'What did you do next?'

'Nothing. Seeing that the lift had arrived, I opened the door and saw the dead body.'

'Did you touch it?'

'Are you kidding? I've got experience with that sort of thing.'

'How did you know the man was dead?'

'As I said, I have experience. So I ran to the green-grocer's and called you, the police. Then I went and stood guard in front of the lift.'

Mrs Cosentino came in with a steaming cup.

'Would you like a little coffee?'

Montalbano accepted and emptied the demitasse. Then he rose to leave.

'Wait a minute,' said the security guard, opening a drawer and handing him a writing pad and ballpoint pen.

'You'll probably want to take notes,' he said in response to the inspector's questioning glance.

'What, are we in school or something?' he replied rudely.

He couldn't stand policemen who took notes. Whenever he saw one doing so on television, he changed the channel.

*

In the apartment next door, Signora Gaetana Pinna, with the tree-trunk legs, was waiting. As soon as she saw Montalbano, she pounced.

'Did you finally take the body away?'

'Yes, signora. You can use the lift now. No, don't close your door. I need to ask you a few questions.'

'Me? I've got nothin' to say.'

He heard a voice from inside the flat, but it wasn't so much a voice as a kind of deep rumble.

'Tanina! Don't be so rude! Invite the gentleman inside!'

The inspector entered another typical living-dining room. Sitting in an armchair, in an undershirt, with a sheet pulled over his legs, was an elephant, a man of gigantic proportions. His bare feet, sticking out from under the sheet, looked like elephant feet; even his long, pendulous nose resembled a trunk.

'Please sit down,' the man said, apparently in a talkative mood, motioning towards a chair. 'You know, when my wife gets bad-tempered like that, I feel like . . . like . . .'

'Trumpeting?' Montalbano couldn't help saying.

Luckily the man didn't understand.

'. . . like breaking her neck. What can I do for you?'

'Did you know Mr Lapècora?'

'I don't know nobody in this building. I been livin' here five years and don't even know a friggin' dog. In five years I ain't even made it as far as the landing. I can't move my legs, takes too much effort. Took three stevedores to get me up here, since I couldn't fit in the lift. They put a sling around me and hoisted me up, like a piano.'

He laughed, rather like a roll of thunder.

'I knew that Mr Lapècora,' the wife cut in. 'Nasty man. He couldn't be bothered to say hello, like it caused him pain.'

'You, signora, how did you find out he was dead?'

'How'd I find out? I had to go out shopping and so I called the elevator, but nothing happened. It wouldn't come. I guessed somebody must've left the door open, which these rude people's always doing 'round here. So I went down on foot and saw the security man standing guard over the body. And after I went shopping, I had to climb back up the stairs and I still haven't caught my breath!'

'So much the better. That way you'll talk less,' said the elephant.

*

THE CRISTOFOLETTI FAMILY said the plaque on the door of
the third apartment, but no matter how hard the inspector
knocked, nobody opened up. He went back to the Cosentino flat and rang the doorbell.

'What can I do for you, Inspector?'

'Do you know if the Cristofoletti family—'

Cosentino slapped himself noisily on the forehead.

'I forgot to tell you! With all this business about the
dead body, it completely slipped my mind. Mr and Mrs
Cristofoletti are both in Montelusa. She, Signora Romilda,
that is, had an operation – woman stuff. They should be
back tomorrow.'

'Thanks.'

'Don't mention it.'

Montalbano took two steps on the landing, turned
around and knocked again.

'What can I do for you, Inspector?'

'Earlier you said you had experience dealing with dead
people. What did you mean?'

'I worked as a nurse for a few years.'

'Thanks.'

'Don't mention it.'

✻

He went down to the fifth floor, where according to Cosentino the lift had been waiting with the already murdered
Aurelio Lapècora inside. Had he perhaps gone up one flight
to meet someone who then knifed him?

'Excuse me, signora, I'm Inspector Montalbano.'

The young housewife who had come to the door — about thirty, very attractive but unkempt — put a finger to her lips, her expression complicit, enjoining him to be quiet.

Montalbano fell silent. What did that gesture mean? Damn his habit of always going about unarmed! Gingerly the young woman stood aside from the door, and the inspector, on his guard and looking all around him, entered a small study full of books.

'Please speak very softly. If the baby wakes up, that's the end, we won't be able to talk. He cries like there's no tomorrow.'

Montalbano heaved a sigh of relief.

'You already know everything, signora, don't you?'

'Yes, Mrs Gullotta, the lady next door, told me,' the woman said, breathing the words in his ear. The inspector found the situation very arousing.

'So you didn't see Mr Lapècora this morning?'

'I haven't been out of the house yet.'

'Where is your husband?'

'In Fela. He teaches at the middle school there. He leaves every morning at six-fifteen sharp.'

He was sorry their encounter had to be so brief. The more he looked at Signora Gulisano — that was the surname on the plaque — the more he liked her. In feminine fashion, she sensed this and smiled.

'Will you stay for a cup of coffee?'

'With pleasure.'

*

The little boy who answered the door to the next apartment couldn't have been more than four years old and was fiercely cock-eyed.

'Who are you, stranger?' he asked.

'I'm a policeman,' Montalbano said, smiling, forcing himself to play along.

'You'll never take me alive,' said the kid, and he shot his water pistol at the inspector, hitting him squarely in the forehead.

The scuffle that followed was brief, and as the disarmed child started to cry, Montalbano cold-bloodedly squirted him in the face, drenching him.

'What is this? What's going on here?'

The little angel's mother, Signora Gullotta, had nothing in common with the young mother next door. As a preliminary measure she slapped her son hard, then she grabbed the water pistol the inspector had let fall to the floor and hurled it out of the window.

'There! That'll put an end to all this aggravation!'

With a heart-rending wail, the little boy ran into another room.

'It's his father's fault, always buying him these toys! He's out of the house all day long, doesn't give a damn, and I'm stuck here to look after that little demon! And what do you want?'

'I'm Inspector Montalbano. Did Mr Lapècora by any chance come up to your apartment this morning?'

'Mr Lapècora? To our apartment? Why would he do that?'

'That's what I'm asking you.'

'I guess I knew the man, but it was never anything more than good morning, good evening . . . Not a word more.'

'Perhaps your husband—'

'My husband never spoke to Lapècora. Anyway, when could he have? The guy's always out. He just doesn't give a damn.'

'Where is your husband?'

'He's out, as you can see.'

'Yes, but where does he work?'

'At the port, at the fish market. He's up at four-thirty in the morning and back at eight in the evening. I'm lucky I ever see him at all.'

An understanding woman, this Mrs Gullotta.

*

On the door to the third and last apartment on the fifth floor was the name PICCIRILLO. The woman who answered the door, a distinguished-looking fifty-year-old, was clearly upset and nervous.

'What do you want?'

'I'm Inspector Montalbano.'

The woman looked away.

'We don't know anything.'

Montalbano immediately smelled a rat. Could this woman have been the reason Lapècora went one flight up?

'Let me in. I still have to ask you some questions.'

Signora Piccirillo gruffly stepped aside to let him in, then led him into a small but pleasant sitting room.

'Is your husband at home?'

'I'm a widow. I live with my daughter, Luigina, who's unmarried.'

'Call her in here, if she's at home.'

'Luigina!'

A jeans-clad girl in her early twenties appeared. Cute but very pale, and literally terrified.

The rat smell grew even stronger, and the inspector decided to go on the attack.

'This morning Mr Lapècora came to see you here. What did he want?'

'No!' said Luigina, almost yelling.

'He didn't, I swear it!' the mother proclaimed.

'What was your relation to Mr Lapècora?'

'We knew him by sight,' said Mrs Piccirillo.

'We haven't done anything wrong,' Luigina whined.

'Well, listen closely: if you haven't done anything wrong, you shouldn't be afraid. We have a witness who claims that Mr Lapècora was on the fifth floor when—'

'But why hold that against us? There are two other families living on this floor who—'

'Stop it!' Luigina exploded, in the throes of an hysterical fit. 'Stop it, Mama! Tell him everything! Tell him!'

'Oh, all right. This morning, my daughter, on her way out for an appointment at the hairdresser's, called the lift, which arrived at once. It must have been stopped at the floor below us, the fourth floor.'

'What time was it?'

'Eight o'clock, five past . . . She opened the door and

saw Mr Lapècora sitting on the floor. When I looked inside the lift – I'd gone out with her to wait for it – the man seemed drunk. He had a bottle of wine, unopened, and, uh . . . it looked like he'd soiled himself. My daughter felt disgusted. She closed the lift door. At that moment it left, somebody downstairs had called it. Well, my daughter has a delicate stomach, and that sight made us both a little queasy. So Luigina came back inside to freshen up, and so did I. Not five minutes later, Mrs Gullotta came and told us that poor Mr Lapècora wasn't drunk at all, but dead! And that's the whole story.'

'No,' said Montalbano. 'That's not the whole story.'

'What did you say? I told you the truth!' the woman said, upset and offended.

'The truth is slightly different and more unpleasant. You both immediately realized the man was dead. But you didn't say anything; you acted as if you'd never seen him at all. Why?'

'We didn't want our names ending up on everyone's lips,' Signora Piccirillo admitted in defeat. Then in a sudden burst of energy, she shouted hysterically: 'We're honest people!'

So these two honest people had left the corpse to be discovered by someone else, perhaps someone less honest. And what if Lapècora hadn't been dead yet? They'd left him there to rot, to save . . . to save what?

He went out, slamming the door behind him, and found Fazio, who was on his way to keep him company, standing before him.

'Here I am, Inspector. If you need anything—'

An idea flashed in his brain.

'Yes, I do need something. Knock on this door. There are two women inside, mother and daughter. Failure to offer assistance. Haul 'em in, and make as much racket as possible. I want everyone in the building to think they've been arrested. Then, when I get back to headquarters, we'll let 'em go.'

*

Upon opening the door, Mr Culicchia, an accountant who lived in the first apartment on the fourth floor, gave the inspector a little push backwards.

'We can't let my wife hear us,' he said, standing outside the doorway.

'I'm Inspector—'

'I know, I know. Did you bring me back my bottle?'

'What bottle?' Montalbano asked in shock, staring at the skinny seventy-year-old, who had assumed a conspiratorial air.

'The one that was next to the dead man, the bottle of Corvo white.'

'Wasn't it Mr Lapècora's?'

'Absolutely not! It's mine!'

'I'm sorry, I don't quite understand. Explain.'

'I went out this morning to go shopping, and when I got back, I opened the lift door, and there was Mr Lapècora inside, dead. I realized it at once.'

'Did you call the lift?'

'Why would I do that? It was already on the ground floor.'

'And what did you do?'

'What could I have done, my boy? I've got injuries to my left leg and right arm. Got shot by the Americans. I had four bags in each hand. I couldn't very well have taken the stairs now, could I?'

'Are you telling me you came up in the lift with the body inside?'

'I had no choice! But then, when the lift stopped at my floor, which was also the deceased's floor, the bottle of wine rolled out of one of my bags. So I opened the door to my apartment, took all the bags inside, and then came back out to get the bottle. But I didn't get back in time; somebody'd called the lift to the next floor up.'

'How is that possible if the door was open?'

'But it wasn't! I'd closed it without thinking! Ah, the mind! At my age one doesn't think so clearly any more. I didn't know what to do. If my wife found out I'd lost a bottle of wine she'd skin me alive. You must believe me, Inspector. She's capable of anything, that woman.'

'Tell me what happened next.'

'The lift passed by in front of me again and went down to the ground floor. So I started going down the stairs. When I finally arrived, bum leg and all, I found the security guard there, who wasn't letting anyone get near. I told him about the wine and he promised he'd mention it to the authorities. Are you the authorities?'

'In a sense.'

'Did the guard mention the bottle of wine to you?'

'No.'

'So what am I supposed to do now? Eh? What am I supposed to do? That woman counts the money I spend!' he complained, wringing his hands.

Upstairs they could hear the desperate voices of the Piccirillo women, and Fazio's imperious commands:

'Down the stairs! On foot! And keep quiet!'

Doors opened, questions were asked aloud from floor to floor.

'Who's been arrested? The Piccirillo girls? Are they being taken away? Are they going to jail?'

When Fazio came within reach, Montalbano handed him ten thousand lire.

'After you've taken them to headquarters, go and buy a bottle of Corvo white and bring it to this gentleman here.'

*

Montalbano's interrogation of the other tenants did not yield any important new information. The only one who said anything of interest was the elementary-school teacher Bonavia, who lived on the third floor. He explained to the inspector that his eight-year-old son Matteo had fallen down and bloodied his nose when getting ready for school. As it wouldn't stop bleeding, he had taken him to Casualty. This was around seven-thirty, and there was no trace of Mr Lapècora, dead or alive, in the lift.

Aside from the lift rides he'd taken as a corpse, two things about the deceased seemed clear to Montalbano:

one, he was a decent man, but decidedly unpleasant; and two, he was killed in the lift, between seven thirty-five and eight o'clock.

Since the murderer had run the risk of being surprised with the corpse in the lift by a tenant, this meant the crime had not been premeditated, but committed on impulse.

It wasn't much to go on. Back at headquarters, the inspector thought about this a little, then glanced at his watch. Two o'clock! No wonder he felt so famished. He called Fazio.

'I'm going to Calogero's for some lunch. If Augello arrives in the meantime, send him to me. And one more thing: post a guard in front of the deceased's apartment. Don't let her in before I get there.'

'Don't let who in?'

'The victim's wife, Mrs Lapècora. Are the Piccirillos still here?'

'Yessir.'

'Send 'em home.'

'What'll I tell them?'

'Tell 'em the investigation is continuing. Let those honest people shit their pants a little.'

THREE

'What can I serve you today?'

'What've you got?'

'For the first course, whatever you like.'

'No first course for me today, I'd rather keep it light.'

'For the main course, I've prepared *alalonga all'agrodolce*, and hake in a sauce of anchovies.'

'Going in for haute cuisine, eh, Calò?'

'Now and then I get the urge.'

'Bring me a generous serving of the hake. Ah, and, while I'm waiting, make me a nice plate of seafood antipasto.'

He was overcome by doubt. Was that a light meal? He left the question unanswered and opened the newspaper. It turned out that the little economic measure the government had promised would not be for fifteen billion lire, but twenty. There were sure to be price increases, petrol and cigarettes among them. The unemployment rate in the south had reached a figure that was better left unmentioned. The Northern League, after their tax revolt, had decided to expel the local prefects, a first step towards secession.

Thirty youths in a town near Naples had gang-raped an
Ethiopian girl. The town was defending them: the black
girl was not only black, but a whore. An eight-year-old boy
had hung himself. Three pushers were arrested, average age
twelve. A twenty-year-old man had blown his brains out
playing Russian roulette. A jealous old man of eighty—

'Here's your appetizer.'

And a good thing too. A few more news items and his
appetite would have been gone. Then eight pieces of hake
arrived, enough to feed four people. They were crying out
their joy – the pieces of hake, that is – at having been
cooked the way God had meant them to be. One whiff
was enough to convey the dish's perfection, achieved by
the right amount of breadcrumbs and the delicate balance
between the anchovies and the whisked egg.

He brought the first bite to his mouth, but did not
swallow it immediately. He let the flavour spread sweetly
and uniformly over his tongue and palate, allowing both
to fully appreciate the gift they'd just been given. Then
he swallowed, and Mimì Augello appeared in front of the
table.

'Sit down.'

Mimì Augello sat down.

'I wouldn't mind a bite myself,' he said.

'Do whatever you want, but don't talk. I'm telling you
as a brother, for your own good. Don't talk for any reason
in the world. If you interrupt me while I'm eating this
hake, I'm liable to wring your neck.'

'Could I have some spaghetti with clams?' Mimì, unfazed, asked Calogero as he was passing by.

'White sauce or red?'

'White.'

While waiting, Augello appropriated the inspector's newspaper and started reading. When the spaghetti arrived, Montalbano had fortunately finished his hake. Fortunately, because Mimì proceeded to sprinkle a generous helping of Parmesan cheese over his plate. Christ! Even a hyena, which, being a hyena, feeds on carrion, would have been sickened to see a dish of pasta with clam sauce covered with Parmesan!

'How did you act with the commissioner?'

'What do you mean?'

'I just want to know if you licked his ass or his balls.'

'What on earth are you thinking?'

'C'mon, Mimì, I know you. You pounced on the case of the machine-gunned Tunisian just to make a good impression.'

'I merely did my duty, since you were nowhere to be found.'

Apparently the Parmesan was not enough, as he added two more spoonfuls, then ground a bit of pepper on top.

'And how did you enter the prefect's office, on your hands and knees?'

'Knock it off, Salvo.'

'Why should I? Since you never miss a single opportunity to stab me in the back!'

'Me? Stab you in the back? Listen, Salvo, if after working for four years with you I had really wanted to stab you in the back, you'd now be running the most godforsaken police station in the most godforsaken backwater in Sardinia, while I would be vice-commissioner at the very least. You know what you are, Salvo? You're a colander that leaks water out of a thousand holes, and all I'm ever doing is trying to plug as many holes as possible.'

He was absolutely right, and Montalbano, having let off some steam, changed his tone. 'Tell me at least what happened.'

'I wrote a report, it's all in there. A large motor trawler from Mazàra del Vallo, the *Santopadre*, with a crew of six including one Tunisian. It was his first time on board, poor guy. The usual scenario, what can I say? A Tunisian patrol boat orders them to stop, the fishing boat refuses, the patrol boat fires. Except that things went a bit differently this time. This time, somebody got killed, and I'm sure the Tunisians are sorrier than anybody about it. Because all they care about is seizing the boat and squeezing a ton of money out of the owner, who then has to negotiate with the Tunisian government.'

'What about ours?'

'Our what?'

'Our government. Don't they come into the picture somewhere?'

'God forbid! They'd make everybody waste an endless amount of time trying to resolve the problem through diplomatic channels. You see, the longer the fishing boat is detained, the less the owner earns.'

'But what do the Tunisian coast guards get out of it?'

'They get a cut, just like the municipal police in some of our towns. Not officially, of course. The captain of the *Santopadre*, who's also the owner, says it was the *Rameh* that attacked them.'

'And what's that?'

'That's the name of a Tunisian motor patrol boat whose commanding officer is notorious for behaving exactly like a pirate. But since somebody got killed this time, our government will be forced to intervene. The prefect asked for a very detailed report.'

'So why did they come and bust our balls instead of dealing directly with Mazàra?'

'The Tunisian didn't die immediately, and Vigàta was the nearest port. At any rate, the poor bastard didn't make it.'

'Did they radio for help?'

'Yes, they hailed the *Fulmine*, a patrol boat that's always riding at anchor in our port.'

'How did you put that?'

'Why, what did I say?'

'You said, "riding at anchor". And you probably wrote that in your report to the prefect. A nitpicker like that, I can already imagine his reaction! You're fucked, Mimì, by your very own hand.'

'And what should I have written?'

' "Moored", Mimì, or "docked". "Riding at anchor" means anchored on the open sea. There's a fundamental difference.'

'Oh, God!'

It was well known that the prefect, who went by the name of Dieterich and hailed from Bolzano, didn't know a caïque from a cruiser, but Augello had swallowed the bait and Montalbano relished his small victory.

'Don't worry about it. So what was the upshot?'

'The *Fulmine* arrived at the scene in less than half an hour, but once there, they didn't find anything. They cruised around a bit in the area, with no results. This is what the Harbour Office learned by radio. When our patrol boat comes back in we'll know a few more details.'

'Bah!' said the inspector, doubtful.

'What's wrong?'

'I don't see why it should be of any concern to us or our government if some Tunisians kill a Tunisian.'

Mimì, mouth agape, just stared at him.

'You know, Salvo, I'm sure I say my share of stupid things, but when you come out with one, it's always a whopper.'

'Bah!' repeated Montalbano, unconvinced he'd said anything stupid.

'So, what about our dead man, the one in the lift? What can you tell me about him?'

'I'm not going to tell you anything. That dead man's mine. You took the Tunisian, I'm taking the guy from Vigàta.'

Let's hope the weather improves, thought Augello. *Otherwise, how's anyone going to put up with this guy?*

*

'Hello, Inspector Montalbano? This is Marniti.'

'What can I do for you, Major?'

'I wanted to let you know that our command has decided – and I agree with them – that the fishing-boat incident should be handled by the Harbour Office of Mazàra. The *Santopadre* should therefore weigh anchor at once. Do your people need to do any further searches on the vessel?'

'I don't think so. But I'm thinking that we, too, ought to abide by the wise decision of your command.'

'I didn't dare ask.'

*

'Montalbano here, Mr Commissioner. Please excuse me if—'

'Any news?'

'No, nothing. I was just having some, uh, procedural doubts. Major Marniti of the Harbour Office phoned me just now to tell me their command has decided that the investigation of the Tunisian who was machine-gunned should be transferred to Mazàra. So I was wondering if we, too—'

'Yes, I see, Montalbano. I think you're right. I'll call my counterpart in Trapani at once and tell him we're stopping the investigation. They've got a vice-commissioner in Mazàra who's really on the ball, if I remember correctly. We'll let them take over everything. Were you handling the case directly yourself?'

'No, my deputy, Inspector Augello, was taking care of it.'

'Tell him we'll be sending the autopsy and ballistics reports to Mazàra. We'll have copies sent to Inspector Augello to keep him informed.'

✶

He kicked open the door to Mimì Augello's office, held out his right arm, clenching the fist and grabbing the forearm with his left hand.

'Here, Mimì.'

'What's that supposed to mean?'

'It means the investigation of the killing on the fishing boat has been transferred to Mazàra. You're left empty-handed, while I've still got my lift murder. One to nothing.'

He felt in a better mood now. In fact, the wind had dropped and the sky was clearing.

✶

Around three in the afternoon, Officer Gallo, guarding the late Lapècora's apartment and awaiting his widow's return, saw the door to the Culicchia flat open up. The accountant approached the policeman and said in a whisper, 'My wife has fallen asleep.'

Informed of this, Gallo didn't know what to say.

'The name's Culicchia, the inspector knows me. Have you eaten?'

Gallo, whose insides were tied in knots from hunger, shook his head 'no'.

Culicchia went back into his apartment and soon returned with a platter on which there was a bread roll, a sizable slice of caciocavallo cheese, five slices of salami, and a glass of wine.

'That's Corvo white. The inspector bought it for me.'

He returned again half an hour later.

'I brought you the newspaper, to help you pass the time.'

*

At seven-thirty that evening, as if on cue, every single balcony or window on the same side of the building as the main entrance was full of people looking out for the return of Signora Antonietta, who still didn't know she'd become a widow. The show was going to be in two parts.

Part one: Signora Antonietta, stepping off the bus from Fiacca, the seven twenty-five, would appear at the top of the street five minutes later, with her usual unsociability and self-possession in full view, and with no idea whatsoever that a bomb was about to explode over her head. This first part was indispensable to a full appreciation of the second (for which the spectators would move quickly away from balconies and windows and onto landings and stairwells): upon hearing from the officer on duty why she couldn't enter her apartment, the widow, now apprised of her widowhood, would begin behaving like the Virgin Mary, tearing out her hair, crying out, beating her breast while being ineffectually restrained by fellow mourners who in the meantime would have promptly come to her aid.

The show never took place.

It wasn't right, the security guard and his wife decided,

for Signora Antonietta to learn of her husband's murder from a stranger's mouth. Dressed for the occasion – he in a charcoal-grey suit, she completely in black – they lay in wait for her near the bus stop. When Signora Antonietta got off, they came forward, their faces now matching the colours of their clothing: he grey, she black.

'What's wrong?' Signora Antonietta asked in alarm.

There is no Sicilian woman alive, of any class, aristocrat or peasant, who, after her fiftieth birthday, isn't always expecting the worst. What kind of worst? Any, so long as it's the worst. Signora Antonietta conformed to the rule.

'Did something happen to my husband?' she asked.

Since she was doing it all herself, the only thing left for Cosentino and his wife was to play supporting roles. They spread their hands apart, looking sorrowful.

And here Signora Antonietta said something that, logically speaking, she shouldn't have said.

'Was he murdered?'

The Cosentinos spread their hands apart again. The widow teetered, but kept her footing.

The people at their windows and balconies therefore witnessed a scene that could only have been a disappointment: Mrs Lapècora walking between Mr and Mrs Cosentino and speaking calmly. She was explaining in great detail the operation that her sister had just undergone in Fiacca.

In the dark as to these developments, Officer Gallo, upon hearing the lift stop at his floor at seven thirty-five, stood up from the stair on which he'd been sitting, reviewing what he was supposed to say to the unhappy woman, and took a step forward. The lift door opened and a man got out.

'Giuseppe Cosentino's the name. Seeing as how Mrs Lapècora is going to have to wait, I'm putting her up at my place. Please inform the inspector. I live on the sixth floor.'

✳

The Lapècora apartment was in perfect order. Living-dining room, bedroom, study, kitchen and bath, nothing out of place. On the desk in the study lay the wallet of the deceased, with all his documents and one hundred thousand lire. Therefore – Montalbano said to himself – Aurelio Lapècora had got dressed to go somewhere he wouldn't need identification, credit or money. He sat down in the chair behind the desk and opened the drawers, one after the other. In the first drawer on the left he found stamps, old envelopes with AURELIO LAPÈCORA INC. / IMPORTAZIONE–ESPORTAZIONE printed on the back, pencils, ballpoint pens, erasers, outdated stamps and two sets of keys. The widow explained that one set was for the house and the other for the office. In the drawer below this one, there were only some yellowed letters bound together with string. The first drawer on the right held a surprise: a brand-new Beretta with two reserve cartridge clips and five boxes of ammunition. Mr Lapècora, if he'd wanted to, could have carried out a massacre. The last drawer contained lightbulbs, razor blades, rolls of string and rubber bands.

41

The inspector told Galluzzo, who had replaced Gallo, to bring the weapon and ammunition to headquarters.

'Then check to see if the pistol was registered.'

A smell of stale perfume, burnt straw in colour, hung aggressively in the air of the study, even though the inspector, upon entering, had thrown the window wide open.

The widow had gone and sat in an armchair in the living room. She seemed utterly indifferent, as if sitting in a railway station waiting room, awaiting her train.

Montalbano also sat down in an armchair, and at that moment the doorbell rang. Signora Antonietta instinctively started to get up, but the inspector stopped her with a gesture.

'Galluzzo, go see who it is.'

The door was opened, they heard some whispering, and the policeman returned.

'There's somebody who lives on the sixth floor says he wants to talk to you. Says he's a security guard.'

Cosentino had put on his uniform; he was on his way to work.

'Sorry to disturb you, but seeing as how something just occurred to me—'

'What is it?'

'You see, after she got off the bus, Signora Antonietta, when she found out her husband was dead, asked us if he'd been murdered. Now, if somebody came to me and told me my wife was dead, I might think of the different ways she could have died, but I would never imagine she'd been murdered. Unless I'd considered the possibility before-hand. I'm not sure if that's clear . . .'

'It's perfectly clear. Thank you,' said Montalbano.

He went back in the living room. Mrs Lapècora looked as if she'd been embalmed.

'Do you have any children, signora?'

'Yes.'

'How many?'

'One son.'

'Does he live here?'

'No.'

'What does he do?'

'He's a doctor.'

'How old is he?'

'Thirty-two.'

'He should be informed.'

'I'll tell him.'

Gong. End of the first round. When they resumed, the widow took the initiative.

'Was he shot?'

'No.'

'Strangled?'

'No.'

'Then how did they manage to kill him in a lift?'

'With a knife.'

'A kitchen knife?'

'Probably.'

The woman got up and went into the kitchen. The

inspector heard her open and close a drawer. She returned and sat back down.

'Nothing missing here.'

The inspector went on the counter attack.

'Why did you think the knife might be yours?'

'Just a thought.'

'What did your husband do yesterday?'

'He did what he did every Wednesday. He went to his office. He used to go there Mondays, Wednesdays and Fridays.'

'What was his schedule?'

'He'd go from ten in the morning to one in the after-noon, then he'd come home for lunch, take a little nap, go back to work at three-thirty and stay there till six-thirty.'

'What would he do at home?'

'He'd sit down in front of the television and not move.'

'And on the days when he didn't go to the office?'

'Same thing, he'd sit in front of the TV.'

'So this morning, today being a Thursday, your husband should have stayed at home.'

'That's right.'

'Instead he got dressed to go out.'

'That's right.'

'Do you have any idea where he was going?'

'He didn't tell me anything.'

'When you left the house, was your husband awake or asleep?'

'Asleep.'

'Don't you think it's strange that, as soon as you went

out, your husband suddenly woke up, got dressed in a hurry, and—'

'He might have got a phone call.'

A clear point in the widow's favour.

'Did your husband still have many business relationships?'

'Business? He shut down the business years ago.'

'So why did he keep going regularly to the office?'

'Whenever I asked him, he'd say he went to watch the flies. That's what he'd say.'

'Would you say that after your husband came home from the office yesterday, nothing out of the ordinary happened?'

'Nothing. At least till nine o'clock in the evening.'

'What happened at nine o'clock in the evening?'

'I took two Tavors. And I slept so soundly that the building could have collapsed on top of me and I still wouldn't have woken up.'

'So if Mr Lapècora had received a phone call or visitor after nine o'clock, you wouldn't have known.'

'Of course not.'

'Did your husband have any enemies?'

'No.'

'Are you sure?'

'Yes.'

'Any friends?'

'One. Cavaliere Pandolfo. They used to phone each other on Tuesdays and then go and chat at the Caffè Albanese.'

'Have you any suspicions as to who might have—'

She interrupted him.

'Suspicions, no. Certainty, yes.'

Montalbano leapt out of the armchair. Galluzzo said 'Shit!' but in a soft voice.

'And who would that be?'

'Who would that be, Inspector? His mistress, that's who. Her name's Karima, with a *K*. She's Tunisian. They used to meet at the office on Mondays, Wednesdays and Fridays. The slut would go there pretending she was the cleaning woman.'

FOUR

The first Sunday of the previous year had fallen on the fifth, the widow said, and that fateful date remained forever etched in her mind.

Anyway, upon coming out of church, where she'd attended Holy Mass at midday, she was approached by Signora Collura, who owned a furniture store.

'Signora, tell your husband that the item he was waiting for arrived yesterday.'

'What item?'

'The sofa bed.'

Signora Antonietta thanked her and went home with a drill boring a hole in her head. What did her husband need a sofa bed for? Although her curiosity was eating her alive, she said nothing to Arelio. To make a long story short, that piece of furniture never arrived at their home. Two Sundays later, Signora Antonietta approached the furniture lady.

'You know, the colour of the sofa bed clashes with the shade of the wall.'

A shot in the dark, but right on target.

'I'm sorry, signora, but he told me he wanted dark green, the same as the wallpaper.'

The back room of the office was dark green. So that's where he had the sofa bed delivered, the shameless pig!

On the thirtieth of June that same year – this date, too, forever etched in her memory – she got her first anonymous letter. She had received three in all, between June and September.

'Could I see them?' Montalbano asked.

'I burned them. I don't keep filth.'

The three anonymous notes, written with letters cut out from newspapers in keeping with the finest tradition, all said the same thing: your husband Arelio is seeing a Tunisian jade named Karima, known by all to be a whore, three times a week, Mondays, Wednesdays and Fridays. The woman went there either in the morning or afternoon on those days. Occasionally she would buy cleaning supplies at a shop on the same street, but everyone knew she was meeting Signor Arelio to do lewd things.

'Were you ever able to . . . verify any of this?' the inspector asked tactfully.

'Do you mean did I ever spy on them to see when the trollop was going in and out of my husband's office?'

'Well, that too.'

'I don't stoop to such things,' the woman said proudly. 'But I managed just the same. A soiled handkerchief.'

'Lipstick?'

'No,' the widow said with some effort, turning slightly red in the face.

'And a pair of underpants,' she added after a pause, turning even redder.

*

When Montalbano and Galluzzo got to Salita Granet, the three shops on that short, sloping street were already closed. Number 28 was a small building, the ground floor raised three steps up from street level, with two more floors above that. To the side of the main door were three nameplates. The first said: AURELIO LAPÈCORA, IMPORT—EXPORT, GROUND FLOOR; the second: ORAZIO CANNATELLO, NOTARY; the third: ANGELO BELLINO, BUSINESS CONSULTANT, TOP FLOOR. Using the keys Montalbano had taken from Lapècora's study, they went inside. The front room was a proper office, with a big nineteenth-century desk made of black mahogany, a small secretarial table with a 1940s Olivetti typewriter on it, and four large metal bookcases overflowing with old files. On the desk was a functioning telephone. There were five chairs in the office, but one was broken and overturned in the corner. In the back room . . . The back room, with its now familiar dark green walls, seemed not to belong to the same apartment. It was sparkling clean, with a large sofa bed, television, telephone extension, stereo system, cocktail trolley with a variety of liqueurs, mini-fridge, and a horrendous female nude, buttocks to the wind, over the couch. Next to the sofa was a small end table with a faux art nouveau lamp on top, its drawer stuffed with condoms of every kind.

'How old was the guy?' Galluzzo asked.

'Sixty-three.'

'Jesus!' said the policeman, giving a whistle of admiration. The bathroom, like the back room, was dark green and glistening, equipped with built-in hairdryer, bath with shower-hose extension, and full-length mirror.

They returned to the front room, rummaged through the desk's drawers, opened a few of the files. The most recent correspondence was more than three years old.

They heard some footsteps upstairs, in the office of the notary, Cannatello. The notary wasn't in, they were told by the secretary, a reed-thin thirtyish young man with a disconsolate expression. He said the late Mr Lapècora used to come to the office just to pass the time. On the days when he was there, a good-looking Tunisian girl would come to do the cleaning. Oh, and, he almost forgot, over the last few months Mr Lapècora had received fairly frequent visits from a nephew, or at least that's how Mr Lapècora introduced him the one time the three had met at the front door. He was about thirty, tall, dark, well-dressed, and he drove a metallic-grey BMW. He must have spent a lot of time abroad, this nephew, because he spoke with an odd sort of accent. No, he couldn't remember anything about the BMW's number plate, hadn't paid any notice.

Suddenly the thin young man assumed the expression of somebody looking at the ruins of his home after an earthquake. He said he had a precise opinion about this crime.

'And what would that be?' asked Montalbano.

It could only have been the usual young lowlife looking for money to feed his drug habit.

They went back downstairs, where Montalbano called Mrs Lapècora from the office phone.

'Excuse me, but why didn't you tell me you have a nephew?'

'Because we don't.'

*

'Let's go back to the office,' Montalbano said when they were just around the corner from headquarters. Galluzzo didn't dare ask why. In the bathroom of the dark green room, the inspector buried his nose in the towel, breathed deeply, then started riffling through the little cupboard beside the sink. He found a small bottle of perfume, called Volupté, and handed it to Galluzzo.

'Here, put some of this on.'

'Where?'

'Up your arse,' came the inevitable reply.

Galluzzo dabbed a drop of Volupté on his cheek, and Montalbano stuck his nose next to it and inhaled. That was it: the very same scent, the colour of burnt straw, that he'd smelled in Lapècora's study. Wanting to be absolutely certain, he repeated the gesture.

Galluzzo smiled.

'Uh, Chief, if anybody saw us ... who knows what they'd think?'

The inspector didn't answer, but walked over to the phone.

'Hello, signora? Sorry to disturb you again. Did your husband use any kind of perfume or cologne? No? Okay, thanks.'

✻

Galluzzo came into Montalbano's office.

'Lapècora's Beretta was registered on the eighth of December of last year. Since he didn't have a licence to carry a gun, he was only allowed to keep it at home.'

Something, the inspector thought, must have been troubling him about that time, if he decided to buy a gun.

'What are we going to do with the pistol?'

'We'll keep it here. Listen, Gallù, here are the keys to the office. I want you to go there early tomorrow morning, let yourself in, and wait there. Try not to let anyone see you. If the Tunisian girl hasn't found out what happened, she should show up tomorrow according to schedule, since it's Friday.'

Galluzzo grimaced.

'It's unlikely she hasn't heard.'

'Why? Who would have told her?'

It looked to the inspector as if Galluzzo was desperately trying to back out.

'I don't know ... Word gets out ...'

'Ah, and I don't suppose you said anything to your brother-in-law the reporter? Because if you did—'

'Inspector, I swear, I haven't told him anything.'

Montalbano believed him. Galluzzo wasn't the type to tell a bare-faced lie.

'Well, you're going to Lapècora's office anyway.'

*

'Montalbano? This is Jacomuzzi. I wanted to notify you of our test results.'

'Oh God, Jacomù, wait a second, my heart is racing. God, what excitement! . . . There, I'm a little calmer now. Please "notify" me, as you put it in your peerless bureaucratese.'

'Aside from the fact that you're an incurable arsehole, the cigarette butt was a common stub of Nazionale without filter; there was nothing abnormal in the dust we collected from the floor of the lift, and as for the little piece of wood—'

'It was only a kitchen match.'

'Exactly.'

'I'm speechless, breathless – in fact, I think I'm about to have a heart attack! You've delivered the murderer to me!'

'Go fuck yourself, Montalbano.'

'It'd still be better than listening to you. What did he have in his pockets?'

'A handkerchief and a set of keys.'

'And what can you tell me about the knife?'

'A kitchen knife, very used. Between the blade and the handle we found a fish scale.'

'Didn't you pursue that any further? Was it a mullet scale or a cod scale? Keep investigating, don't leave me hanging!'

'What is wrong with you anyway?'

'Jacomù, try to use your brains a little. If we were in the Sahara desert and you came to me and said you'd found a fish scale on a knife that had been used to kill a tourist, then the thing might, I say might, mean something. But what the fuck could it possibly mean in a town like Vigàta, where out of twenty thousand inhabitants, nineteen thousand nine hundred and seventy eat fish all the time?'

'And why don't the other thirty?' asked Jacomuzzi, stunned and curious.

'Because they're newborn babies.'

*

'Hello? Montalbano here. Could I please speak with Dr Pasquano?'

'Please hold.'

He had just enough time to start singing: *E te lo vojo dì / che sò stato io . . .*

'Hello, Inspector? The doctor's very sorry, but he's performing an autopsy on the two men found goat-tied in Costabianca. But he said to tell you that as far as your murder victim is concerned, the man was bursting with health and would have lived to be a hundred if somebody hadn't killed him first. A single stab wound, dealt with a firm hand. The incident occurred between seven and eight o'clock this morning. D'you need anything else?'

*

In the fridge he found some pasta with broccoli, which he put in the oven to warm up. As a second course, Adelina had made him some roulades of tuna. Thinking he'd had a light lunch, he felt obliged to eat everything. Then he turned on the television and tuned in to the Free Channel, a good local station where his red-haired, Red-sympathizing friend Nicolò Zito worked. Zito was commenting on the killing of the Tunisian aboard the *Santopadre* as the camera zoomed in on the bullet-riddled wheelhouse and on a dark stain in the wood that was probably blood. All of a sudden Jacomuzzi appeared, kneeling down and looking at something through a magnifying glass.

'Buffoon!' Montalbano shouted, then switched the channel to TeleVigàta, the station where Galluzzo's brother-in-law Prestia worked. Here, too, Jacomuzzi made an appearance, except that he was no longer on the fishing boat; now he was pretending to take fingerprints inside the lift where Lapècora had been murdered. Montalbano cursed the saints, stood up, threw a book against the wall. That was why Galluzzo had been so reticent! He knew that the news had spread but didn't have the courage to tell him. Without a doubt it was Jacomuzzi who'd notified the journalists, so he could show off as usual. He couldn't live without it. The man's exhibitionism reached heights comparable only to what one might find in a mediocre actor or some writer with print runs of a hundred and fifty copies.

Now Pippo Ragonese, the station's political commentator, appeared on the screen. He wanted to talk, he said, about the cowardly Tunisian attack on one of our motor trawlers that had been peacefully fishing in our own territorial waters, which was the same as saying on the sacred soil of our homeland. It wasn't literally soil, of course, being the sea, but it was still our homeland. A less faint-hearted government than the current one in the hands of the extreme left would certainly have reacted more severely to a provocation that—

Montalbano turned off the television.

*

The agitation he felt at Jacomuzzi's brilliant move showed no signs of passing. Sitting on the small veranda that gave onto the beach and staring at the sea in the moonlight, he smoked three cigarettes in a row. Maybe Livia's voice would calm him down enough so he could go to bed and fall asleep.

'Hi, Livia. How are you?'

'So-so.'

'I've had a rough day.'

'Oh, really?'

What the hell was wrong with Livia? Then he remembered their phone call that morning, which had ended on a sour note.

'I called to ask you to forgive me for my boorishness.

But that's not the only reason. If you only knew how much I missed you . . .'

It occurred to him that he might be overdoing it.

'Do you miss me, really?'

'Yes, a lot, really.'

'Listen, Salvo, why don't I catch a plane on Saturday morning? I'll be in Vigàta just before lunchtime.'

He became terrified. Livia was the last thing he needed at the moment.

'No, no, darling, it's such a bother for you . . .'

When Livia got something in her head, she was worse than a Calabrian. She'd said Saturday morning, and Saturday morning it would be. Montalbano realized he'd have to call the commissioner the next day. Goodbye, pasta in squid ink!

*

At about eleven o'clock the next morning, since nothing was happening at headquarters, the inspector headed lazily off to Salita Granet. The first shop on that street was a bakery; it had been there for six years. The baker and his helper had indeed heard that a man who owned an office at number 28 had been murdered, but they didn't know him and had never seen him. As this was impossible, Montalbano became more insistent in his questioning, acting more and more the policeman until he realized that to get to his office from his home, Mr Lapècora would have come up the opposite end of the street. And in fact, at the grocer's at number 26, they did know the late

lamented Mr Lapècora, and how! They also knew the
Tunisian girl, what's-her-name, Karima, good-looking
woman — and here a few sly glances and grins were
exchanged between the grocer and his customers. They
couldn't swear by it, of course, but the inspector could
surely understand, a pretty girl like that, all alone indoors
with a man like the late Mr Lapècora, who carried himself
awfully well for his age . . . Yes, he did have a nephew, an
arrogant punk who sometimes used to park his car right
up against the door to the shop, so that once Signora
Miccichè, who tipped the scales at a good three hundred
pounds, got stuck between the car and the door to the
shop . . . No, the number plate? No. If it had been one of
the old kinds, with PA for Palermo or MI for Milan, that
would have been a different story.

The third and last shop on Salita Granet sold electrical
appliances. The proprietor, a certain Angelo Zircone (as
the sign said outside), was standing behind the counter,
reading the newspaper. Of course he knew the deceased;
the shop had been there for ten years. Whenever Mr
Lapècora passed by — in recent years it was only on
Mondays, Wednesdays and Fridays — he always said hello.
Such a nice man. Yes, the appliance man also used to see
the Tunisian girl, and a fine-looking girl she was. Yes, the
nephew, too, now and then. The nephew and his friend.

'What friend?' asked Montalbano, taken by surprise.

It turned out that Mr Zircone had seen this friend at
least three times. He would come with the nephew, and
the two of them would go to number 28. About thirty,

blondish, sort of fat. That was about all he could tell him.
The number plate? Was he kidding? With these number
plates nowadays you couldn't even tell if someone was a
Turk or a Christian . . . A metallic grey BMW. If he said
any more, he'd be making it up.

The inspector rang the doorbell to Lapècora's office.
No answer. Galluzzo, behind the door, was apparently
trying to decide how to react.

'It's Montalbano.'

The door opened at once.

'The Tunisian girl hasn't shown up yet,' said Galluzzo.

'And she's not going to. You were right, Gallù.'

The policeman lowered his eyes, confused.

'Who leaked the news?'

'Jacomuzzi.'

To pass the time during his stake-out, Galluzzo had
organized himself. Having seized a pile of old issues of
Il Venerdì di Repubblica, the glossy Friday magazine supple-
ment of the Rome daily that Mr Lapècora kept in orderly
stacks on a shelf with fewer files, he had scattered them
across the desktop in search of photos of more or less
naked women. After tiring of looking at these, he had
applied himself to solving a crossword puzzle in a yellowed
old magazine.

'Do I have to stay here all frigging day?' he asked
dejectedly.

'I'm afraid so. You'll have to make the best of it.
Listen, I'm going out the back, to take advantage of Mr
Lapècora's bathroom.'

It wasn't often that nature called so far off schedule for him. Perhaps the rage he'd felt the previous evening upon seeing Jacomuzzi playing the fool on television had altered his digestive rhythms.

He sat down on the toilet seat, heaving his customary sigh of satisfaction, and at that exact moment his mind brought into focus something he'd seen a few minutes earlier but had paid absolutely no attention to.

He leapt to his feet and raced into the next room, holding his trousers and underpants at half-mast in one hand.

'Stop!' he ordered Galluzzo, who, in fright, turned pale as death and instinctively put his hands up.

There it was, right next to Galluzzo's elbow: a black **R** in boldface, carefully cut out of some newspaper. No, not some newspaper, but a magazine: the paper was glossy.

'What is going on?' Galluzzo managed to articulate.

'It might be everything and it might be nothing,' replied the inspector, sounding like the Cumaean sibyl.

He pulled up his trousers, fastened his belt, leaving the zipper down, and picked up the telephone.

'Sorry to disturb you, signora. On what date did you say you received the first anonymous letter?'

'On the thirteenth of June last year.'

He thanked her and hung up.

'Gimme a hand, Gallù. We're going to put all these issues of this magazine in order and see if any pages are missing.'

They found what they were looking for: the 7 June

issue was the only one from which two pages had been torn out.

'Let's keep going,' said the inspector.

The 30 July issue was also missing two pages; the same for 1 September.

The three anonymous letters had been composed right there, in the office.

'Now, if you'll excuse me,' Montalbano said politely.

Galluzzo heard him singing in the bathroom.

FIVE

'Mr Commissioner? Montalbano here. I'm calling to say I'm very sorry, but I can't make it to dinner at your house tomorrow evening.'

'Are you sorry because you won't be able to see us, or because you'll miss the pasta in squid ink?'

'Both.'

'Well, if it's something to do with work, I can't really—'

'No, it's got nothing to do with work ... It's that I'm about to receive an impromptu twenty-four-hour visit from my ...'

Fiancée? That sounded downright nineteenth century to the inspector's ear. Girlfriend? At their age?

'Companion?' the commissioner suggested.

'Right.'

'Miss Livia Burlando must be very fond of you to undertake such a long and tedious journey to see you for just twenty-four hours.'

Never had he so much as mentioned Livia to his superior, who – officially, at least – should have been unaware of her existence. Not even when he was in the hospital, that time he'd been shot, had the two ever met.

'Listen,' said the commissioner, 'why don't you introduce her to us? My wife would love that. Bring her along with you tomorrow evening.'

Saturday's feast was safe.

❈

'Is this the inspector I'm speaking to? In person?'

'Yes, signora, this is he.'

'I wanted to tell you something about the gentleman who was murdered yesterday morning.'

'Did you know him?'

'Yes and no. I never spoke to him. Actually, I only found out his name yesterday, on the TV news.'

'Tell me, signora, do you consider what you have to tell me truly important?'

'I think so.'

'All right. Come to my office this afternoon, around five.'

'I can't.'

'Well, tomorrow, then.'

'I can't tomorrow, either. I'm paralyzed.'

'I see. Then I'll come to you, right away, if you wish.'

'I'm always at home.'

'Where do you live, signora?'

'Salita Granet 23. My name is Clementina Vasile Cozzo.'

❈

Walking down the Corso on his way to the appointment, he heard someone call him. It was Major Marniti, sitting at the Caffè Albanese with a younger officer.

'Let me introduce to you Lieutenant Piovesan, commander of the *Fulmine*, the patrol boat that—'

'Montalbano's the name, pleased to meet you,' said the inspector. But he wasn't pleased at all. He had managed to dump that case. Why did they keep dragging him back in?

'Have a coffee with us.'

'Actually, I'm busy.'

'Just five minutes.'

'All right, but no coffee.'

He sat down.

'You tell him,' Marniti said to Piovesan.

'In my opinion, none of it's true.'

'What's not true?'

'I find the whole story of the fishing boat hard to swallow. We received the *Santopadre*'s Mayday signal at one in the morning; they gave us their position and said they were being pursued by the patrol boat *Rameh*.'

'What was their position?' the inspector enquired in spite of himself.

'Just outside our territorial waters.'

'And you raced to the scene.'

'Actually it should have been up to the *Lampo* patrol boat, which was closer.'

'So why didn't the *Lampo* go?'

'Because an hour earlier, an SOS was sent out by a fishing boat that was taking in water from a leak. The

Lampo radioed the *Tuono* for back-up, and so a big stretch of sea was left unguarded.'

Fulmine, Lampo, Tuono: lightning, flash, thunder. *It's always bad weather for the coastguard*, thought Montalbano. But he said, 'Naturally, they didn't find any fishing boat in trouble.'

'Naturally. And me, too, when I arrived at the scene, I found no trace of the *Santopadre* or the *Rameh*, which, by the way, was certainly not on duty that night. I don't know what to think, but the whole thing stinks to me.'

'Of what?'

'Of smuggling.'

The inspector stood up, threw up his hands and shrugged.

'Well, what can we do? The people in Trapani and Mazàra have taken over the investigation.'

A consummate actor, Montalbano.

✻

'Inspector! Inspector Montalbano!' Somebody was calling him again. Was he ever going to get to see Signora, or Signorina, Clementina before nightfall? He turned around; it was Gallo who was chasing after him.

'What's wrong?'

'Nothing's wrong. I saw you walking by so I called you.'

'Where are you going?'

'Galluzzo phoned me from Lapècora's office. I'm going to buy some sandwiches and keep him company.'

Number 23, Salita Granet, was directly opposite number 28. The two buildings were identical.

*

Clementina Vasile Cozzo was a very well-dressed seventy-year-old lady. She was in a wheelchair. Her apartment was so clean it glistened. With Montalbano following behind, she rolled herself over to a curtained window. She gestured to the inspector to pull up a chair and sit down in front of her.

'I'm a widow,' she began, 'but my son Giulio sees to all my needs. I'm retired; I used to teach at primary school. My son pays for a housekeeper to look after me and my flat. She comes three times a day, in the morning, at midday, and in the evening, when I go to bed. My daughter-in-law, who loves me like a daughter, drops by at least once a day, as does Giulio. I can't complain, except for this one misfortune, which befell me six years ago. I listen to the radio, watch television, but most of the time I read. You see?'

She waved her hand toward two bookcases full of books.

So when was the signora – not signorina, that much was clear – going to get to the point?

'I've just given you this preamble to let you know I'm not some old gossip who spends all her time spying on what others are up to. Still, now and then I do see things I would rather not have seen.'

A cordless phone rang on the shelf below the woman's armrest.

'Giulio? Yes, the inspector's here. No, I don't need anything. See you later. Bye.'

She looked at Montalbano and smiled.

'Giulio was against our meeting. He didn't want me getting mixed up in things that, in his opinion, were no concern of mine. For decades the respectable people here did nothing but repeat that the Mafia was no concern of theirs but only involved the people involved in it. But I used to teach my pupils that the "see-nothing, know-nothing" attitude is the most mortal of sins. So now that it's my turn to tell what I saw, I'm supposed to take a step back?'

She fell silent, sighing. Montalbano was starting to like Clementina Vasile Cozzo more and more.

'You'll have to forgive me for rambling. In my forty years as a schoolteacher, I did nothing but talk and talk. I never lost the habit. Please stand.'

Montalbano obeyed, like a good schoolboy.

'Come here behind me and lean forward; bring your head next to mine.'

When the inspector was close enough to whisper in her ear, the signora raised the curtain.

They were practically inside the front room of Mr Lapècora's office, since the white muslin lying directly against the windowpanes was too light to act as a screen. Gallo and Galluzzo were eating their sandwiches, which were actually more like half-loaves, with a bottle of wine and two paper cups between them. Signora Clementina's window was slightly higher than the one across the street, and by some strange effect of perspective, the two policemen and the various objects in the room looked slightly enlarged.

'In winter, when they had the light on, you could see better,' the woman commented, letting the curtain drop.

Montalbano returned to his chair.

'So, signora, what did you see?' he asked.

Clementina Vasile Cozzo told him.

*

When she'd finished her story and he was already taking his leave, the inspector heard the front door open and close.

'The housekeeper's here,' said Signora Clementina.

A girl of about twenty, short, stocky, and stern-looking, cast a stern glance at the intruder.

'Everything all right?' she asked suspiciously.

'Oh yes, everything's fine.'

'Then I'll go in the kitchen and put the water on,' she said. And she exited, in no way reassured.

'Well, signora, thank you so much . . .' the inspector began, standing up.

'Why don't you stay and eat with me?'

Montalbano felt his stomach blanch. Signora Clementina was sweet and nice, but she probably lived on semolina and boiled potatoes.

'Actually, I have so much to—'

'Pina, the housekeeper, is an excellent cook, believe me. For today she's made *pasta alla Norma*, you know, with fried aubergine and *ricotta salata*.'

'Jesus!' said Montalbano, sitting back down.

'And braised beef for the second course.'

'Jesus!' repeated Montalbano.

'Why are you so surprised?'

'Aren't those dishes a little heavy for you?'

'Why? I've got a stronger stomach than any of these twenty-year-old girls who can happily go a whole day on half an apple and some carrot juice. Or perhaps you're of the same opinion as my son Giulio?'

'I don't have the pleasure of knowing what that is.'

'He says it's undignified to eat such things at my age. He considers me a bit shameless. He thinks I should live on porridge. So what will it be? Are you staying?'

'I'm staying,' the inspector replied decisively.

✻

Crossing the street, he climbed three steps and knocked at the door to the office. Gallo came and opened up.

'I relieved Galluzzo,' he explained. Then, 'Did you come from the office, Chief?'

'No, why?'

'Fazio phoned here asking if we'd seen you. He's looking for you. Says he's got something important to tell you.'

The inspector ran to the phone.

'Sorry to bother you, Inspector, but it seems we have a serious new development. Do you remember, yesterday, you told me to put out an all-points bulletin for this Karima? Well, about half an hour ago, Mancuso of the Immigration

Bureau called me from Montelusa. He says he's managed to find out, purely by chance, where the girl lives.'

'Let's have it.'

'She lives in Villaseta, at 70 Via Garibaldi.'

'I'll be right over, we'll go together.'

✻

At the main entrance to headquarters he was stopped by a well-dressed man of about forty.

'Are you Inspector Montalbano?'

'Yes, but I'm in a rush.'

'I've been waiting for you for two hours. Your colleagues didn't know if you were coming back or not. I'm Antonino Lapècora.'

'The son? The doctor?'

'Yes.'

'My condolences. Come inside. But I can only give you five minutes.'

Fazio appeared.

'Car's ready.'

'We'll leave in five minutes. I have to talk to this gentleman first.'

They went into his office. The inspector asked the doctor to sit down, then sat down himself, behind the desk.

'I'm listening.'

'Well, Inspector, I've been living in Valledolmo, where I practise my profession, for about fifteen years. I'm a paediatrician. I got married in Valledolmo. I mention this merely to let you know that I haven't had a close relationship with my parents for some time. Actually, we've never been very intimate. We always spent the obligatory holidays together, of course, and we used to phone each other twice a month. That was why I was so surprised to receive a letter from my father early last October. Here it is.'

He reached into his jacket pocket, took out the letter, and handed it to the inspector.

My dear Nino,

 I know this letter will surprise you. I have tried to keep you from knowing anything about some business I'm involved in which is threatening to turn very serious. But now I realize I can't go on like this. I absolutely need your help. Please come at once. And don't say anything to Mama about this note. Kisses.

 Papa

'And what did you do?'

'Well, you see I had to leave for New York two days later . . . I was away for a month. When I got back, I phoned Papa and asked him if he still needed my help, and he said no. Then we saw each other in person, but he never brought up the subject again.'

'Did you have any idea what this dangerous business was that your father was referring to?'

'At the time I thought it had to do with the business he'd wanted to reopen in spite of the fact that I was strongly against it. We even quarrelled over it. On top of that, Mama had mentioned he was involved with another woman and was being forced to spend a lot of money—'

'Stop right there. So you were convinced that the help

your father was asking you for was actually some sort of loan?'

'To be perfectly frank, yes.'

'And you refused to get involved, despite the desperate, disturbing tone of the letter.'

'Well, you see—'

'Do you make a good living, Doctor?'

'I can't complain.'

'Tell me something: why did you want me to see the letter?'

'Because the murder put everything in a whole new light. I thought it might be useful to the investigation.'

'Well, it's not,' Montalbano said calmly. 'Take it back and treasure it always. Do you have any children, Doctor?'

'A son, Calogerino. Four years old.'

'I hope you never need him for anything.'

'Why?' asked Dr Antonino Lapècora, bewildered.

'Because, if he's his father's son, you're screwed, sir.'

'How dare you!'

'If you're not out of my sight in ten seconds, I'll have you arrested for the first thing I can think of.'

The doctor fled so quickly he knocked over the chair he'd been sitting on.

Aurelio Lapècora had desperately asked his son for help, and the man decided to put an ocean between them.

*

Until thirty years ago, Villaseta consisted of some twenty houses, or rather cottages, arranged ten on each side of the provincial road between Vigàta and Montelusa. In the boom years, however, the frenzy of construction (which seemed to be the constitutional foundation of our country: 'Italy is a Republic founded on construction work') was accompanied by a road-building fever, and Villaseta thus found itself at the intersection of three high-speed routes, one superhighway, one so-called link, two provincial roads, and two inter-provincial roads. Several of these roads, after a few kilometres of picturesque landscape with guard rails appropriately painted red where judges, policemen, carabinieri, financiers and even prison guards had been killed, often surprised the unwary traveller by suddenly ending inexplicably (or all too explicably) against a hillside so desolate as to feed the suspicion that it had never been trod by human foot. Others instead came to an abrupt halt at the seashore, on beaches of fine blond sand with not a single house as far as the eye could see, not a single boat on the horizon, promptly plunging the unwary traveller into the Robinson Crusoe syndrome.

Having always followed its primary instinct to build houses along any road that might appear, Villaseta thus rapidly turned into a sprawling, labyrinthine town.

'We'll never find this Via Garibaldi!' complained Fazio, who was at the wheel.

'What's the most outlying area of Villaseta?' enquired the inspector.

'The one along the road to Butera.'

'Let's go there.'

'How do you know Via Garibaldi is that way?'

'Trust me.'

He knew he wasn't wrong. He had learned from personal experience that in the years immediately preceding the aforementioned economic miracle, the central area of every town or city had streets named, as dutiful reminders, after the founding fathers of the country (such as Mazzini, Garibaldi, Cavour), the old politicians (Orlando, Sonnino, Crispi), and the classic authors (Dante, Petrarch, Carducci; Leopardi less often). After the boom, the street names changed. The fathers of the country were banished to the outskirts, while the town centres now featured Pasolini, Pirandello, De Filippo, Togliatti, De Gasperi, and the ever-present Kennedy (John, not Bobby, although Montalbano, in a lost village in the Nebrodi Mountains, once ended up in a 'Piazza Elli Kennedy,' that is, a 'Kennedy Brothers Square').

*

In reality, the inspector had guessed right on the one hand and wrong on the other. Right insofar as the centrifugal shift of street names had indeed occurred along the road to Butera; wrong insofar as the streets of that neighbourhood, if you could call it a neighbourhood, were named not after the fathers of the country, but, for reasons unknown, after Verdi, Bellini, Rossini and Donizetti. Discouraged, Fazio decided to ask for directions from an old peasant astride a donkey laden with dried branches. Except that the donkey decided not to stop, and Fazio was forced to coast alongside him in neutral.

'Excuse me, can you tell me the way to Via Garibaldi?'

The old man seemed not to have heard.

'The way to Garibaldi!' Fazio repeated more loudly.

The old man turned round and looked angrily at the stranger.

'Away to Garibaldi? You say, "Away to Garibaldi" with the mess we got on this island? Away? Garibaldi should come back, and fast, and break all these sons of bitches' necks!'

SIX

Via Garibaldi, which they finally found, bordered on a yellow, uncultivated countryside interrupted here and there by the small green patches of stunted kitchen gardens. Number 70 was a little house of unwhitewashed sandstone consisting of two rooms, one above the other. The bottom room had a rather small door with a window beside it; the top room, which featured a balcony, was reached by an external staircase. Fazio knocked on the door. It was soon answered by an old woman wearing a threadbare but clean jellaba. Seeing the two men, she unleashed a stream of Arabic words, frequently punctuated by short, shrill cries.

'Well, so much for that idea!' Montalbano commented in irritation, immediately losing heart (the sky had clouded over a little).

'Wait, wait,' Fazio told the old woman, thrusting his hands palms forward in that international gesture that means 'stop'. The woman understood and fell silent at once.

'Ka-ri-ma?' Fazio asked and, afraid he might not have

pronounced the name correctly, he swayed his hips, stroking a mane of long, imaginary hair. The old woman laughed.

'Karima!' she said, then pointed her index finger towards the room upstairs.

With Fazio in front, Montalbano behind him, and the old woman bringing up the rear and yelling incomprehensibly, they climbed the outside staircase. Fazio knocked, but nobody answered. The old woman started to scream even louder. Fazio knocked again. The woman pushed the inspector firmly aside, walked past him, moved Fazio away as well, planted herself with her back to the door, imitated Fazio's swaying of the hips and stroking of the hair, made a gesture that meant 'gone away', then lowered her right hand, palm down, raised it again, spread her fingers, then repeated the 'gone away' gesture.

'She had a son?' the inspector asked in amazement.

'She left with her five-year-old boy, if I've understood correctly,' Fazio confirmed.

'I want to know more,' said Montalbano. 'Call the Immigration Bureau and have them send us someone who speaks Arabic. On the double.'

Fazio walked away, followed by the old woman, who kept on talking to him. The inspector sat down on a stair, fired up a cigarette, and entered an immobility contest with a lizard.

✳

Buscaìno, the officer who knew Arabic because he was born and raised in Tunisia up to the age of fifteen, was there in less than forty-five minutes. Hearing the new arrival speak her tongue, the old woman became anxious to cooperate.

'She says she'd like to tell her uncle the whole story,' Buscaìno translated for them.

First the kid, now an uncle?

'And who the fuck is that?' asked Montalbano, befuddled.

'Uh, the uncle, that would be you, Inspector,' the policeman explained. 'It's a title of respect. She says Karima came back here around nine yesterday morning, but went out again in a hurry. She says she seemed very upset, frightened.'

'Has she got a key to the upstairs room?'

'Yes,' said the policeman, after asking her.

'Get it from her and we'll have a look.'

As they were climbing the stairs, the woman spoke without interruption, with Buscaìno rapidly translating. Karima's son was five years old; she would leave him with the old woman every day on her way to work; the little boy's name was François; he was the son of a Frenchman who had met Karima when passing through Tunisia.

Karima's room was a model of cleanliness and had a double bed, a cot for the boy behind a curtain, a small table with a telephone and television, a bigger table with four chairs, a dressing table with four small drawers, and an armoire. Two of the drawers were full of photographs. In one corner was a cubbyhole sealed off by a plastic sliding door, behind which they found a toilet, bidet and sink. Here the scent of the perfume the inspector had smelled in Lapècora's study, Volupté, was very strong. Aside from the little balcony, there was also a window on the back wall, overlooking a well-tended garden.

Montalbano picked out a photograph of a pretty, dark-skinned woman of about thirty, with big, intense eyes, holding a little boy's hand.

'Ask her if this is Karima and François.'

'Yes, that's them,' said Buscaìno.

'Where did they eat? I don't see any stove or hot plate here.'

The old woman and the policeman murmured animatedly to each other. Buscaìno then said the little boy always ate with the old woman, even when Karima was at home, which she was, sometimes, in the evening.

Did she receive men?

As soon as she heard the question translated, the old woman grew visibly indignant. Karima was practically a djinn, a holy woman halfway between the human race and the angels. Never would she have done *haram*, illicit things. She sweated out a living as a housemaid, cleaning the filth of men. She was good and generous; for shopping expenses, looking after the boy, and keeping the house in order, she used to give the old woman far more than she ever spent, and never once did she ask for change. As the uncle – Montalbano, that is – was clearly a man of honourable sentiment and behaviour, how could he ever think such a thing about Karima?

'Tell her,' the inspector said while looking at the photographs from the drawer, 'that Allah is great and merciful, but if she's bullshitting me, Allah is going to be very upset, because she'll be cheating justice, and then she'll really be fucked.'

Buscaìno carefully translated, and the old woman shut up as if her spring had come unwound. But then a little key inside her wound her back up, and she resumed speaking uncontrollably. The uncle, who was very wise, was right; he'd seen things clearly. Several times in the last two years, Karima had received visits from a young man who came in a large automobile.

'Ask her what colour.'

The exchange between Buscaìno and the old woman was long and laboured.

'I believe she said metallic grey.'

'And what did Karima and this young man do?'

What a man and woman do, uncle. The woman heard the bed creaking over her head.

Did he sleep with Karima?

Only once, and the next morning he drove her to work in his automobile. But he was a bad man. One night there was a lot of commotion. Karima was shouting and crying, and then the bad man left.

She had come running and found Karima sobbing, her naked body bearing signs of having been hit. Fortunately, François hadn't woken up.

Did the bad man by any chance come to see her last Wednesday evening?

How had the uncle guessed? Yes, he did come, but

didn't do anything with Karima. He only took her away in his car.

What time was it?

It might have been ten in the evening. Karima brought François down to her, saying she'd be spending the night out. And in fact she came back the next morning about nine, then disappeared with the boy.

Was the bad man with her then?

No, she'd taken the bus. The bad man arrived a little later, about fifteen minutes after Karima had left with her son. As soon as he learned the woman wasn't there, he got back in his car and sped away to look for her.

Had Karima told her where she was going?

No, she hadn't said anything. The old woman had only seen them heading on foot towards the old quarter of Villaseta, where the buses stop.

Did she have a suitcase with her?

Yes, a very small one.

He told the old woman to look around. Was there anything missing from the room?

She threw open the doors of the armoire, and the scent of Volupté exploded in the room. She opened a few drawers and rummaged around in them.

When she'd finished, she said that Karima had packed the suitcase with a pair of slacks, a blouse and some panties. She didn't wear bras. She'd also thrown in a change of clothes and some underwear for the boy.

The inspector asked the woman to look very carefully. Was anything else missing?

Yes, the large book she kept next to the telephone.

The book turned out to be some sort of diary or ledger. Karima must certainly have taken it with her.

'She's not planning to stay away very long,' Fazio commented.

'Ask her,' the inspector told Buscaìno, 'if Karima spent the night out often.'

Now and then, not often. But she always let her know.

Montalbano thanked Buscaìno and asked him, 'Could you give Fazio a ride to Vigàta?'

Fazio gave his superior a perplexed look.

'Why, what are you going to do?'

'I'm going to hang around a little longer.'

*

Among the many photographs the inspector began to examine were those in a large yellow envelope, some twenty-odd photos of Karima in the nude, in various poses from provocative to downright obscene, a kind of sampling of the merchandise, which was obviously of the highest quality. How was it a woman like that hadn't succeeded in finding a husband or rich lover to take care of her so she wouldn't have to prostitute herself? There was a shot of a pregnant Karima some time before, gazing lovingly at a tall, blond man and literally hanging from him. Probably François's father, the Frenchman passing through Tunisia. Other photos showed Karima as a little girl with a boy slightly older than her. They bore a strong resemblance, had the same eyes. Brother and sister, no doubt. Actually there were a great many photos of her with her brother, taken over the years. The last must have been the one in which Karima, with her infant son, a few months old, in her arms, stood next to her brother, who was wearing some sort of uniform and holding a sub-machine gun. He took this photograph and went downstairs.

The woman was crushing minced meat in a mortar, folding in grains of cooked wheat. On a platter beside her, all ready to be roasted, were some skewers of meat, with each morsel wrapped in a vine leaf. Montalbano brought his fingertips together, pointing upwards, artichoke-like – *a cacòcciola*, in Sicilian – and shook his hand up and down. The old woman understood the question and, pointing to the mortar, said:

'*Kubba.*'

Then she picked up one of the skewers.

'Kebab,' she said.

The inspector showed her the photo and pointed at the man. The woman answered something incomprehensible. Montalbano felt pissed off at himself. Why had he been in such a hurry to send Buscaìno away? Then he remembered that for years and years the Tunisians had been mixed up with the French. He gave it a try.

'*Frère?*'

The old woman's eyes lit up.

'*Oui. Son frère Ahmed.*'

'*Où est-il?*'

'*Je ne sais pas,*' said the woman, throwing up her hands.

After this exchange straight out of a French conversation

manual, Montalbano went back upstairs and grabbed the photo of the pregnant Karima with the blond man.

'*Son mari?*'

The old woman made a gesture of scorn.

'*Simplement le père de François. Un mauvais homme.*'

She'd met too many of them – bad men, that is – had the beautiful Karima, and was apparently still meeting them.

'*Je m'appelle Aisha,*' the old woman said out of the blue.

'*Mon nom est Salvo,*' said Montalbano.

*

He got in the car, found the pastry shop he'd caught a glimpse of on the way, bought twelve cannoli, and drove back to the house. Aisha had set a table under a tiny pergola behind the cottage, at the front of the garden. The countryside was deserted. Before doing anything else, Montalbano unwrapped the pastry tray, and the old woman immediately ate two cannoli as an appetizer. Montalbano wasn't too thrilled with the *kubba*, but the kebabs had a tart, herbal flavour that made them a little more sprightly, or so, at least, he defined them according to his imperfect use of adjectives.

During the meal Aisha probably told him the story of her life, but she'd forgotten her French and was speaking only Arabic. Nevertheless, the inspector actively participated: when the old woman laughed, he laughed too; when she grew sad, he put on a face fit for a funeral.

When supper was over, Aisha cleared the table, while Montalbano, at peace with himself and the world, smoked a cigarette. When the old woman returned, she was wearing a mysterious, conspiratorial expression. In her hand was a narrow, flat black box that probably once held a necklace or something similar. Aisha opened it, and inside was a savings-account passbook for the Banca Popolare di Montelusa.

'Karima,' the old woman said, bringing her forefinger to her lips, meaning that this was a secret and should remain so.

Montalbano took the booklet from the box and opened it.

An even five hundred million lire.

*

The previous year – Signora Clementina Vasile Cozzo told him – she'd suffered a terrible spell of insomnia she could do nothing about. Luckily it lasted only a few months. She would spend most of the night watching television or listening to the radio. Reading, no. She couldn't read for very long, because after a while her eyes would start to flutter. Once – it must have been around four in the morning, perhaps earlier – she heard the shouts of two drunkards quarrelling right under her window. She opened the curtain, just out of curiosity, and noticed that the light was on in Mr Lapècora's office. What could Mr Lapècora be doing there at that hour of the night? But Mr Lapècora was not there, in fact. Nobody was there; the front room of the office was empty. So Signora Vasile Cozzo concluded that somebody had left the light on.

Suddenly, however, from the other room, which she knew existed but couldn't see from her window, there emerged a young man who used to come to the office now and then, even when Lapècora wasn't there. Stark naked, the man ran to the telephone, picked up the receiver, and started talking. Apparently the telephone had been ringing, though the signora hadn't heard it. Moments later, Karima emerged, also from the back room, and also naked. She stood there listening to the young man, who was growing animated as he spoke. When the telephone call was over, the young man grabbed Karima and they went back into the other room to finish what they'd been doing when they were interrupted by the telephone. They later reappeared fully dressed, turned off the light, and left in the man's large metallic grey car.

Over the course of the previous year this scenario had repeated itself four or five times. For the most part they would stay there for hours not doing or saying anything. If he grabbed her by the arm and took her into the other room, it was only to pass the time. Sometimes he would write or read, and she would doze in the chair, head resting on the table, waiting for the phone to ring. Sometimes, after the call came in, the man would make a call or two himself.

On Mondays, Wednesdays and Fridays, the woman, Karima, would clean the office — but what was there to clean, for Christ's sake? And sometimes she would answer the phone, but she never passed the call on to Mr Lapècora, even when he was right next to her. He would only sit there, listening to her talk, head down and looking at the floor, as if none of it was his concern, or as if he felt offended.

In the opinion of Clementina Vasile Cozzo, the maid, the Tunisian girl, was a bad, evil woman.

Not only did she do what she did with the dark young man, but now and then she would go and wheedle poor old Lapècora, who inevitably would give in, letting himself be led into the back room. One time, when Lapècora was sitting at the little secretarial table reading the newspaper, she kneeled in front of him, unzipped his trousers, and, still kneeling . . .

At this point Signora Vasile Cozzo, blushing, interrupted her narrative.

It was clear that Karima and the young man had keys to the office, whether they had been given them by Lapècora or had copies made themselves. It was also clear, even though there were no insomniac witnesses, that the night before Lapècora was murdered, Karima had spent a few hours in the victim's home. This was proved by the scent of Volupté. Did she also own a set of keys to the flat, or had Lapècora himself let her in, taking advantage of the fact that his wife had taken a generous dose of sleeping pills? In any case, the whole thing seemed not to make sense. Why risk being caught in the act by Mrs Lapècora when they could easily have met at the office? For the hell of it? Just to season an otherwise predictable relationship with the thrill of danger?

And then there was the matter of the three anonymous

letters, unquestionably pieced together in that office. Why had Karima and the dark young man done it? To put Lapècora in a difficult bind? It didn't tally. They had nothing to gain by it. On the contrary, they risked jeopardizing the availability of their telephone number and whatever it was the company had become.

For a better understanding of all this, Montalbano would have to wait for Karima to return. Fazio was right: she must have slipped away to avoid answering dangerous questions and would come back on the sly. The inspector was positive that Aisha would keep the promise she'd made to him. In his unlikely French, he'd explained to her that Karima had got mixed up with a nasty crowd, and that sooner or later that bad man and his friends would surely kill not only her but also François and Aisha herself. He had the impression he'd sufficiently convinced and frightened her.

They agreed that as soon as Karima reappeared, the old woman would phone him; she had only to ask for Salvo and say only her name, Aisha. He left her the telephone numbers to his office and home, telling her to make sure she hid them well, as she had done with the passbook.

Naturally the argument held water on one condition: that Karima was not the killer. But no matter how much he turned it over in his head, the inspector could not picture her with a knife in her hand.

*

He glanced at his watch by the flame of his lighter. Almost midnight. For more than two hours now he'd been sitting on the veranda, in darkness to avoid getting eaten alive by mosquitoes and sand flies, hashing and rehashing what he'd learned from Signora Clementina and Aisha.

Yet he needed one further clarification. Could he possibly call Mrs Vasile Cozzo at that hour? She had told him that every evening the housekeeper, after giving her dinner, would help her undress and put her in the wheelchair. But even if she was ready for bed, she didn't turn in immediately; she would watch television late into the night. She could move from the wheelchair to the bed, and vice versa, by herself.

'Signora, it's unforgivable, I know.'

'Not at all, Inspector, not at all! I was awake, watching a movie.'

'Well, signora. You told me the dark young man sometimes used to read or write. Do you know what it was he read? Or wrote? Could you tell?'

'He used to read newspapers and letters. And he would write letters. But he didn't use the typewriter that was there in the office. He'd bring his own, a portable. Anything else?'

*

'Hi, darling. Were you asleep? No? Are you sure? I'll be at your place tomorrow around one in the afternoon. Don't go out of your way for me, please. I'll just come, and if you're not there, I'll wait. I have the keys, after all.'

SEVEN

Apparently, in his sleep, one part of his brain had kept working on the Lapècora case. Around four o'clock in the morning, in fact, a memory came back to him, and he got up and started searching frantically among his books. Suddenly he remembered that he'd lent the book he was looking for to Augello, after his deputy had seen the film made from it on television. He'd now had it for six months and still hadn't given it back. Montalbano got upset.

'Hello, Mimì? Montalbano here.'

'Ohmygod! What's going on? What happened?'

'Do you still have that novel by Le Carré entitled *Call for the Dead*? I'm sure I lent it to you.'

'What the fuck?! It's four in the morning!'

'So what? I want it back.'

'Salvo, I'm telling you this as a loving brother: why don't you have yourself committed?'

'I want it back immediately.'

'But I was asleep! Calm down. I'll bring it to the office

in the morning. Otherwise I would have to put on my underwear, start looking, get dressed—'

'I don't give a shit. You're going to look for it, find it, get in your car, even in your underwear, and bring it to me.'

He dragged himself about the house for half an hour, doing pointless things like trying to understand the phone bill or reading the label on a bottle of mineral water. Then he heard a car screech to a halt, a dull thud against the door, and the car leaving. He opened the door: the book was on the ground, the lights of Augello's car already far away. He had a mind to make an anonymous phone call to the carabinieri.

Hello, this is a concerned citizen. There's some madman driving around in his underwear . . .

He let it drop. He started leafing through the novel.

The story went exactly as he'd remembered it. Page 8:

'Smiley, Maston speaking. You interviewed Samuel Arthur Fennan at the Foreign Office on Monday, am I right?'

'Yes . . . yes I did.'

'What was the case?'

'Anonymous letter alleging Party membership at Oxford . . .'

And there, on page 139, was the beginning of the conclusion that Smiley would arrive at in his report:

'It was, however, possible that he had lost his heart for his work, and that his luncheon invitation to me was a first step to confession. With this in mind he might also have written the anonymous letter which could have been designed to put him in touch with the Department.'

Following Smiley's logic, it was therefore possible that Lapècora had written the anonymous letters exposing himself. But if he was their author, why hadn't he sent them to the police or carabinieri under some other pretext?

No sooner had he formulated this question than he smiled at himself for being so naive. In the hands of the police or carabinieri, an anonymous letter might have triggered an investigation and have led to far graver consequences for Lapècora. By sending them to his wife, Lapècora was hoping to provoke a reaction of the more domestic variety, but one that would nevertheless rescue him from a situation that was becoming either too dangerous or unbearable. He wanted to pull out, and those were cries for help. But his wife had taken them at face value, that is, as anonymous letters denouncing a tawdry, common liaison. Offended, she had not reacted, but only withdrawn into a scornful silence. And so Lapècora, in despair, had written to his son, this time without hiding behind a veil of anonymity. But the son, blinded by egotism and the fear of losing a few lire, fled to New York.

Thanks to Smiley, it all made sense. He went back to sleep.

*

Commendatore Baldassare Marzachì, director of the Vigàta post office, was notorious for being a presumptuous imbecile. And he didn't fail to live up to his reputation this time, either.

'I cannot grant your request.'

'And why not, if I may ask?'

'Because you don't have a judge's authorization.'

'And why should I need that? Any other employee of your office would have given me the information I asked for. It's of no consequence whatsoever.'

'That's your opinion. Had they given you this information, my employees would have committed a punishable infraction.'

'Commendatore, let's be reasonable. I am merely asking you for the name of the postman who services the neighbourhood in which Salita Granet is located. Nothing more.'

'And I'm not going to tell you, okay? Supposing I did tell you, what would you do?'

'I would ask the postman a few questions.'

'See? You want to violate the postal code of secrecy.'

'What on earth are you talking about?'

An utter nitwit. Which isn't so easy to find these days, now that nitwits disguise themselves as intelligent people. The inspector decided to resort to a bit of high drama that would annihilate his adversary. Without warning, he let his body fall backwards, shoulders planted firmly against the back of the chair, and began shaking his hands and legs, trying desperately to open his shirt collar.

'Oh God,' he gasped.

'Oh God!' echoed Commendator Marzachì, standing up and rushing to the inspector. 'Are you ill?'

'Please help me,' wheezed Montalbano.

The post-office manager bent down, tried to loosen the inspector's collar, and at that moment Montalbano started shouting.

'Let me go! For God's sake, let me go!'

All at once he grabbed Marzachì's hands, and as the commendatore was instinctively struggling to break free, he held them up around his own neck.

'What are you doing?' muttered Marzachì, totally confused, not understanding what was happening. Montalbano yelled again.

'Let me go! How dare you!' he bawled, still clutching the commendatore's hands.

The door flew open, and two terrorized postal employees appeared, a man and a woman, who unmistakably saw their boss trying to strangle the inspector.

'Get out of here!' Montalbano yelled at the two. 'Out! It's nothing! Everything's fine!'

The employees withdrew, closing the door behind them. Montalbano calmly readjusted his collar and glared at Marzachì, who, as soon as he'd released him, had backed up against a wall.

'You're fucked, Marzachì. They saw you, those two. And since they hate you like the rest of your staff, I'm sure they'd be happy to testify. Assaulting a police officer. What shall we do? Do you want to be reported or not?'

'Why do you want to ruin me?'

'Because I hold you responsible.'

'For what, for God's sake?'

'For the worst things imaginable. For letters that take two months to go from one part of Vigàta to another, for packages that arrive torn apart with half the contents missing – and you talk to me of the postal code of secrecy, which you can stick straight up your arse – for books that I wait and wait for and that never come . . . You're a piece of shit that dresses up in dignity to cover this cesspool. Is that enough?'

'Yes,' said Marzachì, shattered.

*

'Yes, of course he used to receive mail. Not a lot, but some. There was one company outside of Italy that used to write to him, but nobody else, really.'

'Where were they from?'

'I never noticed. But the stamps were foreign. I can tell you what the company was called, though, because its name was on the envelope. Aslanidis was the name. I remember it because my dad, rest his soul, who'd fought in Greece, met a girl from those parts whose name was Galatea Aslanidis. Used to talk about her all the time.'

'Did the envelopes say what this company sold?'

'Yes. *Dattes*, they said. Dates.'

*

'Thanks for coming so quickly,' said Signora Antonietta Palmisano, lately become the widow Lapècora, as soon as she opened the door for Montalbano.

'Why? Did you want to see me?'

'Yes. Didn't they tell you I phoned your office?'

'I haven't been there yet today. I came here on my own.'

'Then it's a case of kleptomania,' the woman concluded.

For a moment the inspector felt confused; then he understood that she'd intended to say 'clairvoyance'.

One of these days I'll introduce her to Catarella, he thought, *then I'll transcribe the dialogue. Better than Ionesco!*

'What did you want to see me about, signora?'

Antonietta Palmisano Lapècora mischievously wagged a small forefinger.

'No, no, no. You have to talk first, since you thought to come on your own.'

'Signora, I would like you to show me exactly what you did the other morning when you were getting ready to go out to see your sister.'

The widow was dumbfounded, opening and closing her mouth.

'Is this some kind of joke?'

'Hardly.'

'Are you asking me to put on my nightgown?' said Signora Antonietta, blushing.

'I wouldn't dream of it.'

'Well, let me think. I got out of bed as soon as the alarm went off. Then I took—'

'No, signora, perhaps I didn't make myself clear enough.

I don't want you to *tell* me what you did, I want you to *show* me. Let's go in the other room.'

They went into the bedroom. The armoire was wide open, a suitcase full of women's dresses on the bed. On one of the bedside tables was a red alarm clock.

'Do you sleep on this side of the bed?' asked Montalbano.

'Yes. What should I do, lie down?'

'No need. Just sit on the edge.'

The widow obeyed, but then:

'What's any of this got to do with Arelio's murder?' she asked.

'Please do as I say, it's important. Just five minutes and I'll be out of your hair. Tell me: did your husband also wake up when the alarm went off?'

'Normally he slept lightly. His eyes would pop open if I made the slightest noise. But now that you've made me think back on it, that morning he didn't hear the alarm. In fact, he must have had a bit of a cold, a stuffed-up nose, because he started snoring, which he hardly ever did.'

A terrible actor, poor old Lapècora. But it worked, at least that time.

'Go on.'

'I got up, picked up the clothes I'd put on that chair over there, and went into the bathroom.'

'Let's move.'

Embarrassed, the woman led the way. When they were in the bathroom, Signora Antonietta, looking at the floor, asked, 'Do I have to do everything?'

'Of course not. You were dressed when you came out of the bathroom, correct?'

'Yes, fully dressed, that's how I always do it.'

'Then what did you do?'

'I went into the dining room.'

Having learned her lesson by now, she walked towards the dining room, followed by the inspector.

'I picked up my purse, which I'd prepared on this couch the night before, then I opened the door and went out on the landing.'

'Are you sure you locked the door behind you when you went out?'

'Absolutely certain. I called the lift—'

'That'll be enough, thank you. What time was it, do you remember?'

'Six twenty-five. I was late, actually, so late that I started running.'

'What was the snag?'

The woman gave him a questioning look.

'For what reason were you running late? Let me put it another way. If someone knows he has to go somewhere the next morning, he usually sets the alarm clock, calculating the amount of time it will take to—'

Signora Antonietta smiled.

'A callus on my foot was hurting,' she said. 'I put on some ointment, wrapped it up, and lost some time I hadn't allowed for.'

'Thanks again, and sorry for the disturbance. Goodbye.'

'Wait! Where are you going? Are you leaving?'

'Oh, yes, of course. You had something to tell me.'

'Sit down a minute.'

Montalbano did as she said. In any case, he'd found out what he wanted to know: that is, the widow Lapècora had not entered the study, where Karima almost certainly had been hiding.

'As you can see,' the woman began, 'I'm getting ready to leave. As soon as I can give Arelio a proper funeral, I'm going away.'

'Where will you go, signora?'

'To stay with my sister. She has a big house, and she's sick, as you know. I'll never set foot in Vigàta again, even after I'm dead.'

'Why not go and live with your son?'

'I don't want to inconvenience him. And I don't get along with his wife, who spends money like water while my poor son is always complaining that he can't make ends meet. Anyway, what I wanted to tell you was that, when I was going through some old stuff I don't need anymore and want to throw away, I found the envelope the first anonymous letter came in. I thought I'd burned it, but I must have destroyed only the letter. And since you seemed particularly interested . . .'

The address had been typed.

'May I keep this?'

'Of course. Well, that's all.'

She stood up, as did the inspector, but then she went over to the sideboard, picked up a letter that was lying on it, and shook it at Montalbano.

'Look at this, Inspector. Arelio's been dead barely two days and already I have to start paying the debts he ran up with his filthy little arrangements. Just yesterday I received – apparently the post office already knows he was killed – I received two bills from the office. One for electricity: two hundred and twenty thousand lire! And one for the phone: three hundred and eighty thousand! But he wasn't the one using the phone, you know. Who would he ever call anyway? It was that Tunisian whore who was phoning, that's for sure, probably calling her family in Tunisia. Then this morning, this came. God only knows what kinds of ideas that dirty slut put into my idiot husband's head!'

So compassionate, the widow Antonietta Lapècora, née Palmisano. The envelope had no stamp on it; it had been hand-delivered. Montalbano decided not to show too much curiosity, only as much as was necessary.

'When was this brought here?'

'This morning, as I said. A bill for one hundred and seventy-seven thousand lire, from the Mulone printing works. Incidentally, Inspector, could you give me back the keys to the office?'

'Do you need them right away?'

'Not right this instant. But I'd like to start showing it to people who might be interested in buying it. I want to sell the apartment too. I've already worked out that the funeral alone is going to cost me over five million lire between one thing and the next.'

Like mother, like son.

'With the proceeds from the office and the apartment,' said Montalbano in a fit of malice, 'you could pay for twenty funerals.'

*

Empedocle Mulone, owner of the print shop, said yes, the late Mr Lapècora had indeed ordered some stationery with slightly different letterhead from the old one. Signor Arelio had been coming to him for twenty years, and they were friends.

'How was it different?'

'It said "Import-Export" instead of "Importazione-Esportazione." But I advised him against it.'

'He shouldn't have made the change?'

'I didn't mean the letterhead, but the idea of restarting the business. He'd already been retired about five years, but things are different now. Businesses are failing. It's a bad time. And you know what he did, instead of thanking me for the advice? He got pissed off. He said he read the newspapers and watched TV, and so he knew what the situation was.'

'Did you send the parcel with the printed matter to his home or his office?'

'He asked me to send it to the office, and that's what I did, on one of the weekdays when he was there. I don't remember the exact date, but if you want—'

'Never mind.'

'The bill, on the other hand, I sent to the missus, since

I guess Mr Lapècora can't very well make it to the office now, can he?'

And he laughed.

✳

'Here's your espresso, Inspector,' said the barman at the Caffè Albanese.

'Totò, listen. Did Mr Lapècora sometimes come here with his friends?'

'Sure! Every Tuesday. They'd talk and play cards. Always the same group.'

'Give me their names.'

'All right. Let's see: Pandolfo, the accountant—'

'Wait. Give me the phone book.'

'No need to call him on the phone. He's the elderly gentleman sitting at that table over there, eating an ice.'

Montalbano took his demitasse and went over to the accountant.

'May I sit down?'

'Absolutely, Inspector.'

'Thanks. Do we know each other?'

'You don't know me, sir, but I know you.'

'Mr Pandolfo, did you play cards with the deceased very often?'

'Often? We played every Tuesday. Because, you see, every Monday, Wednesday, and—'

'Friday he was at the office,' said Montalbano, completing the now familiar refrain.

'What would you like to know?'

'Why did Mr Lapècora decide to go back into business?'

Pandolfo looked sincerely surprised.

'Go back into business? When did he ever do that? He never talked about it with us. But we all knew he went to the office out of habit, just to pass the time.'

'Did he ever mention the maid, a certain Karima, who used to come and clean the office?'

There was a darting of the eyes, an imperceptible hesitation that would have gone unnoticed had Montalbano not been keeping the man squarely in his sights.

'The man had no reason to tell me about his cleaning woman.'

'Did you know Lapècora well?'

'Whom can you say you know well? Some thirty years ago when I lived in Montelusa, I had a friend, a smart man, bright, witty, sharp, sensible. He had it all. And he was generous, too, a real angel. If anyone was in need, they could have anything he owned. Then one evening his sister left her baby boy with him, not six months old. He was supposed to look after him for two hours or so, maximum. As soon as the sister left, the guy picked up a knife, chopped the baby up and boiled him in a pot with a sprig of parsley and a clove of garlic. I'm not kidding, you know. I'd been with the man that same day, and he'd been the same as always, smart, polite. So, to get back to poor old Lapècora, yeah, I knew him, all right, enough to see that he'd really changed over the last two years.'

'In what way?'

'Well, he became nervous, never laughed. In fact, he'd pick a fight and make a big to-do over the smallest things.'

'Any idea what might have been the cause?'

'One day I asked him about it. It was a health problem, he said. The first stages of arteriosclerosis, that's what his doctor told him.'

✳

The first thing he did in Lapècora's office was sit down at the typewriter. He opened the drawer to the little secretarial table and found some stationery printed with the old letterhead and yellowed with age. He took out a sheet, reached into his coat pocket, and removed the envelope that Signora Antonietta had given him. He copied its address on the typewriter. A foolproof test if there ever was one. The *r*'s jumped above the line, the *a*'s dropped below, and the *o* was a little black ball. The address on the anonymous letter's envelope had been written on this same typewriter.

He looked outside. Signora Vasile Cozzo's housekeeper, standing on a stepladder, was cleaning the windows. He opened the window and called out.

'Hello! Is the signora there?'

'Wait,' said the girl, giving him a dirty look. Clearly she wasn't very fond of the inspector.

She stepped down from the ladder, disappeared, and a short while later Signora Clementina's head appeared just above the sill. There was no need for them to raise their voices so much, as they were less than ten yards away from each other.

'Excuse me, signora, but if I'm not mistaken, you told me that, sometimes, the young man, do you remember . . .?'

'Yes, the young man.'

'You said he used to type sometimes. Is that right?'

'Yes, but he didn't use the office typewriter. He would bring his own portable.'

'Are you sure? Might it have been a computer?'

'No, it was a portable typewriter.'

What kind of idiotic way to conduct an investigation was this? He suddenly realized the two of them must look like a couple of old housewives gossiping across their balconies.

After saying goodbye to Clementina, to regain some semblance of dignity in his own eyes he began a detailed search of the office like a true professional, looking for the parcel the printer had sent. But he never found it; nor did he find a single envelope or sheet of paper with the new letterhead in English.

They'd removed everything.

As for the portable typewriter Lapècora's bogus nephew used to bring along instead of using the office machine, he thought he'd come up with a plausible explanation for this. The young man had no use for the keyboard of the old Olivetti. Apparently, he needed one with a different alphabet.

EIGHT

He left the office, got in his car, and drove to Montelusa. At Customs Police headquarters, he asked for Captain Aliotta, who was his friend. They let him in immediately.

'It's been so long since we spent an evening together! I'm not blaming you. It's my fault, too,' said Aliotta, embracing Montalbano.

'Let's forgive each other and try to rectify the situation soon.'

'Okay. What can I do for you?'

'I need the name of that sergeant of yours I spoke to on the phone last year, the one who gave me that precious information about the supermarket in Vigàta. The case of the weapons traffic, remember?'

'Of course. His name's Laganà.'

'Could I speak with him?'

'What's it about?'

'He would have to come to Vigàta for half a day at the most, I think. I'd like him to examine the files of a business owned by that guy who was murdered in a lift.'

'I'll call him for you.'

Sergeant Laganà was a burly fifty-year-old with a crew cut and gold-rimmed glasses. Montalbano took an immediate liking to him.

He explained in great detail what he wanted from him and gave him the keys to Lapècora's office. The sergeant looked at his watch.

'I can be in Vigàta at three o'clock this afternoon, if the captain has no objection.'

∗

Just to be thorough, once the inspector had finished chatting with Aliotta, he asked if he could use his phone and phoned headquarters, where he hadn't shown his face since the previous evening.

'Chief, is that really you yourself?'

'Cat, it's really me myself. Been any calls?'

'Yessir, Chief. Two for Inspector Augello, one for—'

'Cat, I don't give a fuck about other people's phone calls!'

'But you asked me yourself just now!'

'All right, Cat: have there been any phone calls personally for me myself?'

By making the necessary linguistic adjustments, maybe he would get a sane answer.

'Yessir, Chief. There was one. But it didn't make sense.'

'What do you mean, it didn't make sense?'

'I couldn't understand anything. But I think they were relatives.'

'Whose relatives?'

'Yours, Chief. They called you by your first name: Salvo, Salvo.'

'Then what?'

'Then they sounded like they were in pain, or sneezing or something. They said: 'Aiee . . . sha! Aiee . . . sha!''

'Wait, who was "they"? Was it a man or a woman?'

'An old woman, Chief.'

Aisha! He dashed out the door, forgetting to say goodbye to Aliotta.

*

Aisha was sitting in front of her house, upset and weeping. No, Karima and François had not shown up; she'd called him for another reason. She stood up and led him inside. The room had been turned upside down; they'd even gutted the mattress. Want to bet they'd taken the bank book? No, that they didn't find, Aisha said reassuringly.

Upstairs, where Karima lived, it was even worse. Some flagstones had been torn out of the floor; one of François's toys, a little plastic truck, was in pieces. The photographs were all gone, including the ones advertising Karima's charms. *A good thing I took a few myself*, the inspector thought. But they must have made a tremendous racket. Where had Aisha run off to in the meantime? She hadn't run off, the old woman explained. The previous day she'd gone to see a friend in Montelusa. It got late, and so she slept over. A stroke of luck: if they'd found her at home, they would certainly have cut her throat. They must have had keys;

neither of the doors, in fact, had been forced. Surely they'd come for the photos; they wanted to erase the very memory of what Karima looked like.

Montalbano told the old woman to gather her things together. He was going to take her himself to her friend's house in Montelusa. She would have to remain there for a few days, just to be safe. Aisha glumly agreed to go. The inspector explained that while she was getting ready, he was going out to the nearest tobacco shop and would be back in ten minutes at most.

*

A short distance before the tobacco shop, in front of the Villaseta primary school, there was a noisy gathering of gesticulating mothers and weepy children. They were laying siege to two municipal policemen from Vigàta who'd been seconded to Villaseta and whom Montalbano knew. He drove on, bought his cigarettes, but on the way back, curiosity got the better of him. He pushed through the crowd, invoking his authority, deafened by the shouting.

'They bothered you about this bullshit too?' asked one of the policemen in amazement.

'No, I just happened to be passing by. What's going on?'

The mothers, who heard his question, answered all at once, with the result that the inspector understood nothing.

'Quiet!' he yelled.

The mothers fell silent, but the children, now terrified, started wailing even louder.

'The whole thing's ridiculous, Inspector,' said the same policeman as before. 'Apparently, since yesterday morning, there's been some little kid attacking the other kids on their way to school. He steals their food and then runs away. He did the same thing this morning.'

'Looka here, looka here,' one mother butted in, showing Montalbano a little boy with eyes puffy from being punched. 'My son din't wanna give 'im 'is omelette, and so 'e 'it 'im! An' 'e really 'urt 'im!'

The inspector bent down and stroked the little boy's head.

'What's your name?'

''Ntonio,' said the little boy, proud to have been the one chosen from the crowd.

'Do you know this boy who stole your omelette?'

'No sir.'

'Is there anyone here who recognized him?' the inspector asked in a loud voice. There was a chorus of 'No.'

Montalbano leaned back down to 'Ntonio.

'What did he say to you? How did you know he wanted your omelette?'

'He spoke foreign. I din't unnastand. So he pulled off my backpack and opened it. I tried to take it back, but he punched me, twice, and he grabbed my omelette sandwich and ran away.'

'Continue the investigation,' Montalbano ordered the two police officers, managing by some miracle to keep a straight face.

*

At the time of the Muslim domination of Sicily, when Montelusa was called Kerkent, the Arabs built a district, on the outskirts of town, where they lived by themselves. When the Muslims later fled in defeat, the Montelusians moved into their homes and the name of the district was Sicilianized into Rabàtu. In the second half of the twentieth century, a tremendous landslide swallowed it up. The few houses left standing were damaged and lopsided, remaining upright by absurd feats of equilibrium. When they returned, this time as paupers, the Arabs moved back into that part of town, replacing the roof tiles with sheet metal and using partitions of heavy cardboard for walls.

It was to this quarter that Montalbano accompanied Aisha with her paltry bundle of belongings. The old woman, still calling him 'uncle', wanted to kiss and embrace him.

✻

It was three o'clock in the afternoon and Montalbano, who hadn't had time to eat, was in the throes of a gut-twisting hunger. He went to the Trattoria San Calogero and sat down.

'Is there anything left to eat?'

'For you, sir, there's always something.'

At that exact moment he remembered about Livia. She'd completely slipped his mind. He rushed to the phone, trying feverishly to think of an excuse. Livia had said she'd be there by lunchtime. She was probably furious.

'Livia, darling.'

'I just got here, Salvo. The flight left two hours late, with no explanation. Were you worried, darling?'

'Of course I was worried,' Montalbano lied shamelessly, realizing the winds were favourable. 'I've been phoning home every fifteen minutes without any answer. A little while ago I decided to call the airport, and they told me the flight was two hours late. That finally set my mind at rest.'

'Sorry, love, but it wasn't my fault. When are you coming home?'

'Unfortunately I can't right now. I'm in the middle of a meeting in Montelusa; I'll be at least another hour I'm sure. Then I'll come running. Oh, and listen: tonight we're going to the commissioner's for dinner.'

'But I didn't bring anything to wear!'

'You can go in jeans. Have a look in the fridge, Adelina must have cooked something.'

'No, that's all right. I'll wait for you, we can eat together.'

'I've already made do with a sandwich. I'm not hungry. See you soon.'

He sat back down at his table, where a pound of mullet awaited him, fried to a delicate crisp.

*

A little weary from her journey, Livia had gone to bed. Montalbano got undressed and lay down beside her. They kissed. Suddenly Livia pulled away and started sniffing him.

'You smell like fried food.'

'Of course I do. I just spent an hour interrogating some guy in a fried-food shop.'

They made love calmly, knowing they had all the time in the world. Then they sat up in bed, pillows behind their heads, and Montalbano told her the story of Lapècora's murder. Thinking he was amusing her, he told her how he'd had Mrs Piccirillo and her daughter, who set such great store by their honour, brought in to the station. He also told her he'd had Fazio buy a bottle of wine for Mr Culicchia, who'd lost his when it rolled next to the corpse. Instead of laughing, as Montalbano expected, Livia looked at him coldly.

'Arsehole,' she said.

'I beg your pardon?' Montalbano asked with the aplomb of an English lord.

'You're an arsehole and a sexist. First you disgrace those two wretched women, and then you buy a bottle of wine for the guy who had no qualms about riding up and down in the lift with a corpse. Now tell me that's not acting like a jerk.'

'Come on, Livia, don't look at it that way.'

Unfortunately Livia insisted on looking at it that way. It was six o'clock before he managed to appease her. To distract her he told her the story of the little boy who was stealing other children's late-morning snacks.

But Livia didn't laugh this time, either. In fact, she seemed to turn melancholy.

'What's wrong? What did I say? Did I do something wrong again?'

'No, I was just thinking of that poor little boy.'

'The one who got beaten up?'

'No, the other one. He must be really famished and desperate. You say he didn't speak Italian? He's probably the child of some immigrants who can't even put food on the table. Or maybe he was abandoned.'

'Jesus Christ!' cried Montalbano, thunderstruck by the revelation, yelling so loudly that Livia gave a start.

'What's got into you?'

'Jesus Christ!' the inspector repeated, eyes bulging out of his head.

'What on earth did I say?' Livia asked, concerned.

Without answering, Montalbano dashed to the phone, completely naked.

'Catarella, get the fuck off the line and get me Fazio at the double. Fazio? In one hour, at the latest, I want you all at the office. Got that? All of you. If anybody's missing, I'll be furious.'

He hung up, then dialled another number.

'Commissioner? Montalbano here. I'm embarrassed to say, but I can't make it to dinner tonight. No, it's not because of Livia. It's got to do with work. I'll explain everything. Lunch tomorrow? By all means. And please give your wife my apologies.'

Livia had got out of bed, trying to understand how her words could have provoked such a frantic reaction.

Montalbano's only answer was to throw himself on the bed, dragging her along with him. His intentions were perfectly clear.

'But didn't you say you'd be at the office in an hour?'

'Fifteen minutes more or less, what's the difference?'

*

Crammed into Montalbano's office, which was certainly not spacious, were Augello, Fazio, Tortorella, Gallo, Germanà, Galluzzo and Grasso, who had begun working at the station less than a month ago. Catarella stood leaning against the door frame, an ear to the switchboard. Montalbano had brought along a reluctant Livia.

'But what am I going to do there?'

'Believe me, you might be very useful.'

But he hadn't given her a single word of explanation.

In utter silence, he drew a rough but sufficiently precise street map of Villaseta, which he then showed to all present.

'This is a little house on Via Garibaldi in Villaseta. No one is living there at the moment. Here behind it is a garden . . .'

He went on to illustrate every detail, the neighbouring houses, the main junctions, the smaller crossroads. He had committed everything to memory the previous afternoon, when alone in Karima's room. With the exception of Catarella, who would remain on duty at headquarters, they were all to have a part in the operation. Using the map, the inspector pointed out the position that each was to take up. He ordered them to arrive at the scene one by one: no sirens, no uniforms — in fact, no police cars at all. They were to remain absolutely inconspicuous. If anybody wanted to bring his own car, he must leave it at least half a kilometre away from the house. They could bring along whatever they wanted, sandwiches, coffee, beer, because it was probably going to take a long time. They might have to lie in wait all night, and there wasn't even any guarantee of success. Most likely the person they were looking for wouldn't show up. When the street lights came on, that would signal the start of the operation.

'Weapons?' asked Augello.

'Weapons? What weapons?' Montalbano muttered, momentarily bewildered.

'I don't know, but since it seemed like something serious, I thought—'

'Who is it we're looking to capture?' Fazio cut in.

'A snack thief.'

Everyone in the room seemed to stop breathing. Beads of sweat appeared on Augello's forehead.

I've been telling him for the last year he should have his head examined, he thought.

*

It was a clear, moonlit night, windless and still. It had only one flaw, in Montalbano's eyes. It seemed as if time didn't want to pass. Every minute was mysteriously expanding, dilating into five more.

By the light of a cigarette lighter, Livia had put the gutted mattress back on the bed frame, lain down, and gradually fallen asleep. She was now sleeping in earnest.

The inspector, seated in a chair beside the window that looked over the back, had a clear view of the garden and the surrounding countryside. Fazio and Grasso were supposed to be in that area, but no matter how hard he squinted, he could see no trace of them. They were probably hidden among the almond trees. He felt pleased with his men's professionalism; they'd embraced the assignment wholeheartedly after he told them the little boy was probably François, Karima's son. He took a drag on his fortieth cigarette and glanced at his watch by the faint glow. He decided to wait another half hour, after which he would tell his men to go back home. At this exact moment he noticed a very slight movement at the point where the garden ended and the countryside began; but, more than a movement, it was a momentary break in the reflection of the moon on the straw and yellow scrub. It couldn't have been Fazio or Grasso. He had purposely wanted to leave that area unguarded, as if to favour, even suggest, that approach. The movement, or whatever it was, repeated itself, and this time Montalbano could make out a small, dark shape coming slowly forward. It was the kid, no doubt about it.

He moved slowly toward Livia, guided by her breath.

'Wake up, he's coming.'

He returned to the window and was joined at once by Livia. Montalbano spoke into her ear:

'As soon as they catch him, I want you to go immediately downstairs. He's going to be terrified, but when he sees a woman he might feel reassured. Stroke him, kiss him, tell him whatever you can think of.'

The little boy was right next to the house now. They

could see him clearly as he raised his head and looked up towards the window. Suddenly a man's shape appeared, descended on the boy and grabbed him. It was Fazio.

Livia flew down the stairs. François, kicking, let out a long, heart-rending wail, like an animal caught in a trap. Montalbano turned on the light and leaned out of the window.

'Bring him upstairs. You, Grasso, go and round up the others.'

Meanwhile the child's wailing had stopped and turned into sobbing. Livia was holding him in her arms, talking to him.

*

He was still very tense but had stopped crying. Eyes glistening and ardent, he studied the faces around him, slowly regaining confidence. He was sitting at the same table where, only a few days before, he had sat with his mother beside him. This, perhaps, was why he clung to Livia's hand and didn't want her to leave him.

Mimì Augello, who had briefly absented himself, returned with a bag in his hand. Everyone immediately realized he'd been the only one with the right idea. Inside were some ham sandwiches, bananas, cookies and two cans of Coca-Cola. As a reward, Mimì received an emotional glance from Livia, which naturally irritated Montalbano. The deputy inspector stammered, 'I had somebody prepare it last night . . . I thought that, if we were dealing with a hungry little boy . . .'

As he was eating, François gave in to fatigue and fell asleep. He didn't manage to finish the cookies. All at once his head fell forward onto the table, as if someone had turned off a switch inside him.

'So where do we take him now?' asked Fazio.

'To our house,' Livia said decisively.

Montalbano was struck by that 'our'. And as he was gathering up a pair of jeans and a T-shirt for the little boy, he couldn't tell whether he should be pleased or upset.

The child didn't open his eyes once during the ride back to Marinella, or when Livia undressed him after making up a bed for him on the living-room sofa.

'What if he wakes up and runs away while we're asleep?' asked the inspector.

'I don't think he will,' Livia reassured him.

Montalbano, in any case, wasn't taking any chances. He closed the window, lowered the shutters, and gave the front-door key two turns.

They too went to bed. But despite how tired they were, it took them a long time to fall asleep. The presence of François, whom they could hear breathing in the next room, made them both inexplicably uneasy.

*

Around nine o'clock the next morning, very late for him, the inspector woke up, got quietly out of bed so as not to disturb Livia, and went to check on François. The boy wasn't there. Not on the couch, nor in the bathroom. He'd escaped, just as the inspector had feared. But how the hell did he do it, with the front door locked and the shutters still down? He started looking everywhere the child might be hiding. Nothing. Vanished. He had to wake Livia and tell her what had happened, get her advice. He reached out and at that moment saw the child's head resting against his woman's breast. They were sleeping in each other's arms.

NINE

'Inspector? Sorry to bother you at home. Could we meet this morning? I'd like to give you my report.'

'Certainly. I'll come to Montelusa.'

'No, that's all right. I'll come down to Vigàta. Shall we meet in an hour at the office in Salita Granet?'

'Yes, thanks, Laganà.'

*

He went into the bathroom, trying to make as little noise as possible. Also to avoid disturbing Livia and François, he put on his clothes from the previous day, which were additionally rumpled from the night-long stake-out. He left a note: there was a lot of stuff in the fridge, he'd be back by lunchtime. As soon as he'd written it, he remembered that the commissioner had invited them for lunch. That was out of the question now, with François there. He decided to phone at once, otherwise he might forget. He knew that the commissioner spent Sunday mornings at home, except in extraordinary circumstances.

'Montalbano? Don't tell me you're not coming for lunch!'

'Unfortunately I can't, Mr Commissioner, I'm sorry.'

'Is it something serious?'

'Quite. The fact is, early this morning, I became – I don't know how to put this – sort of a father.'

'Congratulations!' was the commissioner's reply. 'So, Miss Livia ... I can't wait to tell my wife, she'll be so happy. But I don't understand how this would prevent you from coming. Ah, I get it: the event is imminent.'

Flummoxed by his superior's misapprehension, Montalbano recklessly proceeded to entangle himself in a long, tortuous, stammering explanation that jumbled together murder victims and children's snacks, Volupté perfume and the Mulone printing works. The commissioner gave up.

'All right, all right, you can explain it all later. Listen, when is Miss Livia leaving?'

'Tonight.'

'So we won't have the pleasure of meeting her. Too bad. It'll have to wait till next time. Tell you what, Montalbano: when you think you'll have a couple of free hours, give me a ring.'

Before going out, he went to take a last look at Livia and François, who were still asleep. Who would ever break their embrace? He frowned, gripped by a dark premonition.

*

The inspector was astonished to find everything in Lapè-cora's office exactly as he had left it. Not one sheet of paper out of place, not a single clip where he hadn't seen it last time. Laganà had understood.

'It wasn't a search, Inspector. There was no need to turn the place upside down.'

'So, what can you tell me?'

'Well, the business was founded by Aurelio Lapècora in 1965. He'd worked as a clerk before that. The business was involved in importing tropical fruit and had a warehouse in Via Vittorio Emanuele Orlando, near the port, equipped with cold-storage rooms. They exported cereals, chickpeas, broad beans, pistachios, things of that sort. The volume of business was decent, at least until the second half of the eighties. Then things went steadily downhill. To make a long story short, in January of 1990, Lapècora was forced to liquidate, but it was all above board. He even sold the warehouse and made a tidy profit. His papers are all on file. An orderly man, this Lapècora. If I'd had to do an inspection here, I wouldn't have found anything wrong. Four years later, also in January, he obtained authorization to reopen the business, which was still incorporated. But he never bought another depository or warehouse, nothing whatsoever. And you know what?'

'I think I already know. You found no trace of any business transaction from 1994 to the present.'

'Right. If Lapècora only wanted to come and spend a few hours at the office – I'm referring to what I saw in the next room – what need was there to reconstitute the business?'

'Find any recent post?'

'No, sir. All the post's at least four years old.'

Montalbano picked up a yellowed envelope that had been lying on the desk and showed it to the sergeant.

'Did you find any envelopes like this, but new, with the words "Import-Export" in the return address?'

'Not a single one.'

'Listen, Sergeant. Last month a local print shop sent Lapècora a parcel of stationery to this office. Since you found no trace of it, do you think it's possible the whole stock got used up in four weeks?'

'I wouldn't think so. Even when things were going well, he couldn't have written that many letters.'

'Did you find any letters from a foreign firm called Aslanidis, which exports dates?'

'Nothing.'

'And yet, according to the postman, some were delivered here.'

'Did you search Lapècora's home, Inspector?'

'Yes. There's nothing related to his new business there. You want to know something else? According to a very reliable witness, on certain nights, when Lapècora wasn't here, this place was buzzing with activity.'

He proceeded to tell him about Karima and the dark young man posing as a nephew, who used to make and receive phone calls and write letters, but only on his own portable typewriter.

'I get it,' said Laganà. 'Don't you?'

'I do, but I'd like to hear your idea first.'

'The business was a cover, a front, the receiving end of

some kind of illegal trafficking. It certainly wasn't used to import dates.'

'I agree,' said Montalbano. 'And when they killed Lapè-cora, or the night before, they came here and got rid of everything.'

✳

He dropped in at headquarters. Catarella was at the switch-board, working on a crossword puzzle.

'Tell me something, Cat. How long does it take you to solve a puzzle?'

'Ah, they're hard, Chief, really hard. I been workin' on this one for a month and I still can't get it.'

'Any news?'

'Nothing serious, Chief. Somebody arsoned Sebastiano Lo Monaco's parking garage by setting fire to it. The firemen went and put it out. Five motor vehicles got roasted. Then somebody shot at somebody by the name of Filippo Quarantino but they missed and got the window of the house where Mrs Saveria Pizzuto lives and she got so scared she had to go to casualty. Then there was another fire, an arson fire for sure. But just little shit, Chief, kid stuff, nothin' important.'

'Who's in the office?'

'Nobody, Chief. They're all out taking care of these things.'

Montalbano went into his office. On the desk was a parcel wrapped in the paper of the Pipitone pastry shop. He opened it: cannoli, cream puffs, *torroncini*.

'Catarella!'

'At your orders, Chief.'

'Who put these pastries here?'

'Inspector Augello did. He says he bought 'em for the little boy from last night.'

How thoughtful and attentive to abandoned children Mr Mimì Augello had suddenly become! Was he hoping for another glance from Livia?

The telephone rang.

'Chief? It's His Honour Judge Lo Bianco. He says he wants to speak personally with you.'

'Put him on.'

A couple of weeks earlier, Judge Lo Bianco had sent the inspector a complimentary copy of the first tome, all seven hundred pages, of a work to which he'd been devoting himself for years: *The Life and Exploits of Rinaldo and Antonio Lo Bianco, Masters of Jurisprudence at the University of Girgenti at the Time of King Martin the Younger (1402–1409)*. He'd got it in his head that these Lo Biancos were his ancestors. Montalbano had leafed through the book one sleepless night.

'Hey, Cat, are you going to put the judge on the line or not?'

'The fact is, Chief, I can't put him on the line, seeing as he's already here personally in person.'

Cursing, Montalbano rushed to the door, showed the judge into his office, and expressed his apologies. He already felt guilty towards the judge for having phoned him only once about the Lapècora murder, after which he'd completely forgotten he existed. No doubt he'd come to give him a tongue-lashing.

'Just a quick hello, my dear Inspector. Thought I'd drop in, since I was passing by on my way to see my mother who's staying with friends at Durrueli. Let's give it a try, I said to myself. And I was lucky: here you are.'

And what the hell do you want from me? Montalbano said to himself. Given the solicitous glance the judge cast his way, it didn't take him long to figure it out.

'You know, Judge, lately I've been losing sleep.'

'Really? Why's that?'

'I spend the nights reading your book. It's more gripping than a mystery novel, and so rich in detail.'

A lethal bore: dates upon dates, names upon names. By comparison, the train timetable had more surprises and plot twists.

He remembered one episode recounted by the judge in which Antonio Lo Bianco, on his way to Castrogiovanni on a diplomatic mission, fell from his horse and broke a leg. To this insignificant event the judge devoted twenty-two maniacally detailed pages. To show he'd actually read the book, Montalbano foolishly quoted from it.

And so Judge Lo Bianco engaged him for two hours, adding other details as useless as they were minute. When he finally said goodbye, the inspector felt a headache coming on.

'Oh, and listen, dear boy, don't forget to keep me posted on the Lacapra case.'

When he got to Marinella, neither Livia nor François were there. They were down by the water, Livia in her bathing suit and the boy in his underpants. They'd built an enormous sandcastle and were laughing and talking. In French, of course, which Livia spoke as well as Italian. Along with English. Not to mention German, truth be told. The house ignoramus was he, who barely knew three or four words of French he'd learned in school.

He set the table, then looked in the fridge and found the *pasta 'ncasciata* and veal roulade from the day before. He put them in the oven at low heat, then quickly got undressed, put on his swimming trunks, and joined the other two. The first things he noticed were a little bucket, a shovel, a sand-sifter and some moulds in the shapes of fish and stars. He, of course, didn't have such things about the house, and Livia certainly hadn't bought them, since it was Sunday. And there wasn't a soul on the beach aside from the three of them.

'What are those?'

'What are what?'

'The shovel, the bucket—'

'Augello brought them this morning. He's so sweet! They belong to his little nephew, who last year . . .'

He didn't want to hear any more. He dived into the sea, infuriated.

When they returned to the house, Livia noticed the cardboard tray full of pastries.

'Why did you buy those? Don't you know sweets are bad for children?'

'Yes I do, it's your friend Augello who doesn't know it. *He* bought them. And now you're going to eat them, you and François.'

'While we're at it, your friend Ingrid called, the Swedish woman.'

Thrust, parry, counterthrust. And what was the meaning of that 'while we're at it'?

Those two liked each other, that was clear. It had started the previous year, when Mimì had driven Livia around in his car for an entire day. And now they were picking up where they'd left off. What did they do when he wasn't there? Trade cute little glances, smiles, compliments?

They began eating, with Livia and François murmuring to each other from time to time, enclosed inside an invisible bubble of complicity from which Montalbano was utterly excluded. The delicious meal, however, prevented him from getting as angry as he would have liked.

'Excellent, this *brusciuluni*,' he said.

'What did you call it?'

'*Brusciuluni*. The roulade.'

'You nearly frightened me. Some of your Sicilian words . . .'

'You Ligurians don't kid around either. Speaking of which, what time does your flight leave? I think I can drive you to Palermo.'

'Oh, I forgot to tell you. I cancelled my reservation and called Adriana, a colleague of mine, and asked her to fill in for me. I'm going to stay a few more days. It suddenly dawned on me that if I'm not here, who are you going to leave François with?'

The dark premonition he'd had that morning, when he saw them sleeping in each other's arms, was beginning to take shape. Who would ever pry those two apart?

'You seem displeased . . . I don't know . . . irritated.'

'Me? Come on, Livia!'

*

As soon as they'd finished eating, the little boy's eyelids started to droop; he was sleepy and must still have been quite worn out. Livia took him into the bedroom, undressed him, and put him to bed.

'He told me something,' she said, leaving the door ajar.

'Tell me.'

'When we were building the sandcastle, at a certain point he asked me if I thought his mother would ever return. I told him I didn't know anything about what had happened, but I was sure that one day his mother would come back for him. He twisted up his face, and I didn't say any more. A little while later, he brought it up again and said he didn't think she was coming back. Then he dropped the subject. That child is darkly aware of something terrible. Then all of a sudden he started talking again. He told me that that morning, his mother had come home in a rush and seemed frightened. She told him they had to go away. They ran to the centre of Villaseta; his mother told him they had to catch a bus.'

'A bus for where?'

'He doesn't know. While they were waiting, a car drove up. He knew it well; it belonged to a bad man who would sometimes beat his mother. Fahrid.'

'What's the name?'

'Fahrid.'

'Are you sure?'

'Absolutely. He even told me that, when you write it, there's an *h* between the *a* and the *r*.'

So Mr Lapècora's dear young nephew, the owner of the metallic grey BMW, had an Arab name.

'Go on.'

'This Fahrid then got out of the car, grabbed Karima's arm, and tried to force her to get in. She resisted and shouted to François to run away. The boy fled; Fahrid was too busy with Karima and had to choose. François found a hiding place and was too terrified to come out. He didn't dare go back to a woman he called his grandma.'

'Aisha.'

'He got so hungry he had to rob other children of their schooltime snacks to survive. At night he would go up to the house, but he found it all dark and was afraid that Fahrid was lying in wait for him there. He slept outside. He felt hunted like an animal. The other night he couldn't stand it any longer; he had to go back home at all costs. That's why he came so close to the house.'

Montalbano remained silent.

'Well, what do you think?' she asked.

'I think we've got an orphan on our hands.'

Livia blanched; her voice began to tremble.

'Why do you think that?'

'Let me explain the opinion I've formed of the whole affair thus far, also based on what you've just told me. Five years ago, more or less, this attractive, beautiful Tunisian woman comes to our country with her baby boy. She looks for work as a cleaner and has no trouble finding it, because, among other things, she grants favours, upon request, to older men. That's how she meets Lapècora. But at a certain point this Fahrid enters her life. He's probably a pimp or something similar. Fahrid then comes up with a scheme to force Lapècora to reopen his old import-export business as a front for some sort of shady dealings, probably drugs or prostitution. Lapècora, who's basically an honest man, senses that something's not right and gets scared. He tries to wiggle out of a nasty situation by rather ingenuous means. Just imagine, he writes anonymous letters to his wife denouncing himself. Things go on this way for a while, but at a certain point, and I don't know why, Fahrid is forced to clear out. At this point, however, he has to eliminate Lapècora. He arranges for Karima to spend a night at Lapècora's house, hiding in his study. Lapècora's wife has to go to Fiacca the following day, to visit her sister who's sick. Karima had probably filled Lapècora's brain with visions of wild sex in the marriage bed when the wife was away. Who knows? Early the next morning, after Mrs Lapècora has left, Karima opens the front door and lets in Fahrid, who then kills the old man. Lapècora may have attempted to escape; perhaps that was why he was found in the lift. Except that, based on what you just told me, Karima must not have known that Fahrid intended to kill him. When she sees that her accomplice has stabbed Lapècora, she flees. But she doesn't get very far; Fahrid tracks her down and kidnaps her. In all probability, he later kills her, to keep her from talking. And the proof of this is that he went back to Karima's place to remove all the photos of her. He didn't want her to be identified.'

Silently, Livia started crying.

✢

He was alone. Livia had gone to lie down next to François. Montalbano, not knowing what to do, went and sat on the veranda. In the sky, two seagulls were engaged in some sort of duel; on the beach, a young couple were strolling, exchanging a kiss from time to time, but wearily, as if following a script. He went back inside, picked up the last novel written by the late Gesualdo Bufalino, the one about a blind photographer, and went back out on the veranda. He glanced at the cover, the jacket flaps, then closed it. He was unable to concentrate. He could feel an acute malaise slowly growing inside him. And suddenly he understood the reason.

It was merely a foretaste, an advance instalment, of the quiet, familial Sunday afternoons that awaited him, perhaps not even in Vigàta but in Boccadasse. With a little boy who, upon awakening, would call him Papa and ask him to play . . .

Panic seized him by the throat.

TEN

He had to run away at once, to flee the familial ambushes awaiting him in that house. As he got in his car, he couldn't help but smile at the schizophrenic attack he was suffering. His rational side told him he could easily control the new situation, which in any case existed only in his imagination; his irrational side was spurring him to flee, just like that, without a thought.

He arrived in Vigàta and went to his office.

'Any news?'

Instead of answering, Fazio asked another question:

'How's the kid?'

'Fine,' he replied, slightly annoyed. 'Well?'

'Nothing serious. An unemployed man went into a supermarket with a big stick and started smashing up the shelves—'

'Unemployed? You mean there are still people without work in our country?'

Fazio looked stunned.

'Of course there are, Chief. Didn't you know?'

'Frankly, I didn't. I thought everyone had work these days.'

Fazio was clearly at sea.

'And how are they supposed to find this work?'

'By repenting, Fazio. Turning state's witness against the Mafia. This unemployed bloke smashing up supermarket shelves, he's not out of work, he's an arsehole. Did you arrest him?'

'Yes.'

'Go and tell him, on my behalf, that he should turn state's witness.'

'For what case?'

'Anything! Tell him to make something up. But he has to say he's repented. Any bullshit he feels like saying. Maybe you can suggest something to him. But as soon as he turns state's witness, he's set for life. They'll pay him, find him a house, send his kids to school. Tell him.'

Fazio eyed him in silence. Then he said, 'Chief, it's a beautiful day, and still you're in a filthy mood. What gives?'

'None of your goddamn business.'

*

The owner of the shop where Montalbano usually supplied himself with *càlia e simenza* had devised an ingenious system for getting around the obligatory Sunday closing. He would set up a well-stocked booth in front of the lowered shutter.

'Got fresh-roasted peanuts here, nice and hot,' the shopkeeper informed him.

The inspector had him add twenty or so to his *coppo*, the paper cornet already half-full of chickpeas and pumpkin seeds.

His solitary, ruminating stroll to the tip of the eastern jetty lasted longer than usual this time, until after sunset.

*

'This child is extremely intelligent!' Livia said excitedly as soon as she saw Montalbano enter the house. 'I taught him how to play draughts just three hours ago, and now look: he's already beat me once and is about to win again.'

The inspector remained standing beside them, watching the final moves of the game. Livia made a devastating mistake and François gobbled up her two remaining chips. Consciously or unconsciously, Livia had wanted the kid to win; if she'd been playing him instead of François, she would have fought tooth and nail to deny him the satisfaction of victory. Once she even stooped to pretending she'd fainted, letting all the pieces fall to the floor.

'Are you hungry?'

'I can wait, if you want,' the inspector replied, complying with her implicit request to delay supper.

'We'd love to go for a little walk.'

She and François, naturally. The idea that he might wish to tag along never even crossed her mind.

Montalbano set the table grandly, and when he finished he went into the kitchen to see what Livia had made. Nothing. An arctic desolation. The dishes and cutlery sparkled, uncontaminated. Lost in her preoccupation with

François, she hadn't even thought to make dinner. He drew up a rapid, unhappy inventory: as a first course, he could make a little pasta with garlic and oil; as a second course, he could throw something together using sardines in brine, olives, caciocavallo cheese and canned tuna. The worst, in any case, would come the following day, when Adelina, showing up to clean the house and cook, found Livia there with a little boy. The two women didn't take to each other. Once, because of certain comments Livia had made, Adelina had abruptly dropped everything, half finished, to return only after she was certain her rival was gone and already hundreds of miles away.

It was time for the evening news. He turned on the television and tuned into TeleVigàta. On the screen appeared the chicken-arse mug of Pippo Ragonese, their editor. Montalbano was about to change the channel when Ragonese's first words paralysed him.

'What is going on at Vigàta police headquarters?' the newsman asked himself and the entire universe in a tone that would have made Torquemada, in his best moments, seem like he was telling jokes.

He went on to say that in his opinion, Vigàta these days could be compared to the Chicago of the Prohibition era, with all its shoot-outs, robberies and arson. The life and liberty of the common, honest citizen were in constant danger. And did the viewers know what that overrated Police Inspector Montalbano, in the midst of this tragic situation, was working on? The question mark was so emphatically underscored that the inspector thought he could actually see it superimposed on the man's chicken-arse face. Having caught his breath, the better to express due wonder and indignation, Ragonese then stressed every syllable 'On-chas-ing-af-ter-a-snack-thief!'

But he wasn't working on this alone, our inspector. He'd dragged all his men along with him, leaving police headquarters unprotected, with only a sorry switchboard operator on duty. How did he, Ragonese, come to learn of this seemingly comical but surely tragic situation? Needing to speak with Assistant Inspector Augello to get some information, he had telephoned the central police station, only to receive the extraordinary answer given him by the switchboard operator. At first, he'd thought it must be a joke, a tasteless one to be sure, and so he'd insisted. Yet in the end he understood that it was not a prank, but the incredible truth. Did the viewers of Vigàta realize what sort of hands they were in?

'What have I ever done to deserve Catarella?' the inspector asked himself bitterly as he changed channel.

On the Free Channel's news programme, they were broadcasting images of the funeral, in Mazàra, of the Tunisian fisherman machine-gunned to death aboard the trawler *Santopadre*. At the end of the report, the speaker commented on the Tunisian's misfortune to have died so tragically his first time out on the fishing boat. Indeed, he had only just arrived in town, and hardly anyone knew him. He had no family, or at least hadn't had the time to bring them to Mazàra. He was born thirty-two years ago in Sfax, and his name was Ben Dhahab. They showed a photo of him, and at that moment Livia and the little boy walked in, back from their stroll. Seeing the face on the television screen, François smiled and pointed a small finger.

'*Mon oncle*' he said.

Livia was about to tell Salvo to turn off the television because it bothered her when she was eating; for his part, Montalbano was about to reproach her for not having prepared anything for supper. Instead they just stood there dumbstruck, forefingers pointing at each other, while a third forefinger, the little boy's, still pointed at the screen. It was as if an angel had passed, the one who says 'Amen', and everyone remains just as they were. The inspector pulled himself up and sought confirmation, doubting his scant understanding of French.

'What'd he say?'

'He said: "my uncle",' replied a very pale Livia.

When the image vanished from the screen, François took his place at the table, anxious to start eating and in no way disturbed by having seen his uncle on TV.

'Ask him if the man he just saw is his uncle uncle.'

'What kind of idiotic question is that?'

'It's not idiotic. They called me "uncle," too, even though I'm nobody's uncle.'

François answered that the man he'd just seen was his uncle uncle, his mother's brother.

'He has to come with me, right away.'

'Where do you want to take him?'

'To headquarters. I want to show him a photograph.'

'Forget it. Nobody's going to steal your photograph.

François has to eat first. Afterwards, I'm going to come with you; you're liable to lose the boy along the way.'

The pasta came out overcooked, practically inedible.

*

At headquarters there was only Catarella, who, upon seeing the makeshift little family and the look on his superior's face, took fright.

'All peaceable and quiet-like here, Chief.'

'But not in Chechnya.'

The inspector opened a drawer and took out the photos he'd lifted from Karima's house. He selected one and showed it to François. The boy, without a word, brought it to his lips and kissed his mother's image.

Livia barely suppressed a sob. There was no need to ask any questions; the resemblance between the man shown on television and the uniformed man with Karima in the photo was obvious. But the inspector asked anyway.

'Is this *ton oncle?*'

'*Oui.*'

'*Comment s'appelle-t-il?*'

Montalbano felt pleased with his French, like a tourist at the Eiffel Tower or the Moulin Rouge.

'Ahmed,' said the little boy.

'*Seulement* Ahmed?'

'Oh, *non.* Ahmed Moussa.'

'*Et ta mère? Comment s'appelle?*'

'Karima Moussa,' said François, shrugging his shoulders at the obviousness of the question.

Montalbano poured out his anger at Livia, who was not expecting the violent assault.

'What the fuck! You're with the child day and night, you play with him, teach him draughts, but it never occurs to you to find out his name! All you had to do was ask! And that fucking arsehole Mimì! The big investigator! He brings the little bucket, the little shovel, the little sand moulds, the little pastries, and instead of talking to the kid he only talks to you!'

Livia didn't react. Montalbano immediately felt ashamed of his outburst.

'Forgive me, Livia. I'm on edge.'

'I can see.'

'Ask him if he's ever met this uncle in person, even recently.'

Livia and the boy spoke to each other softly. Livia then explained that he had not seen him recently, but that when François was three, his mother had taken him to Tunisia, and there he'd met his uncle along with some other men. But his memory of all this wasn't very clear; he'd mentioned it only because his mother had spoken to him about it.

Therefore, Montalbano concluded, there had been a sort of summit two years earlier, in which, in some way, the fate of poor Mr Lapècora had been decided.

'Listen. Take François to see a movie. There's still time to make the last showing. Then come back here. I've got some work to do.'

*

'Hello, Buscaìno! Montalbano here. I've just found out the full name of the Tunisian woman who lives in Villaseta. Remember?'

'Of course. Karima.'

'Her name is Karima Moussa. Could you do a check there at your own office, at the Immigration Bureau?'

'Are you joking, Inspector?'

'No, I'm not. Why?'

'What? How can you ask me such a thing, with all your experience?'

'Explain yourself.'

'Look, Inspector, even if you were to tell me her parents' names, her grandparents' names on both sides, and her date and place of birth—'

'Pea soup?'

'What else would you expect? They can pass all the laws they want in Rome, but here Tunisians, Moroccans, Libyans, Cape Verdians, Senegalese, Nigerians, Rwandans, Albanians, Serbs and Croats come and go as they please. We're in the blasted Colosseum here: there aren't any doors. The fact that we found this Karima's address the other day is not in the normal order of things. It belongs to the realm of the miraculous.'

'Well, try anyway.'

＊

'Montalbano? What's this business about you chasing after somebody who steals snacks from children? Is he some kind of maniac?'

'No, no, Mr Commissioner. He was a little boy who was starving and so he started robbing schoolchildren of their morning snacks. That's all.'

'What do you mean, that's all? I'm well aware that every now and then you, how shall I say, go off on a tangent. But this time, frankly, I think—'

'Mr Commissioner, I assure you it won't happen again. It was absolutely necessary that we catch him.'

'Did you?'

'Yes.'

'And what did you do with him?'

'I brought him home with me. Livia's looking after him.'

'Are you mad, Montalbano? You must give him back to his parents at once!'

'He hasn't got any. He may be an orphan.'

'What do you mean, "may be"? Do a search, for God's sake!'

'I am. But François—'

'Who on earth is that?'

'The little boy; that's his name.'

'He's not Italian?'

'No, he's Tunisian.'

'Listen, Montalbano, let's drop it for the moment, I'm too confused. But I want you to come to my office tomorrow morning and explain everything to me.'

'I can't, I have to go out of Vigàta. It's very important, believe me. I'm not trying to slip away.'

'Then we'll see each other in the afternoon. I'm serious;

don't let me down. I need you to provide me with a line of defence; Chamber Deputy Pennacchio is here...'

'The one charged with criminal association with mafiosi?'

'The very same. He's preparing a motion to be sent to the Minister of the Interior. He wants your head.'

Indeed. It was Montalbano himself who had initiated the investigation of the honourable deputy.

✢

'Nicolò? Montalbano here. I need to ask a favour of you.'

'So what else is new? Fire away.'

'Are you going to be much longer at the Free Channel?'

'I have to do the midnight report and then I'm going home.'

'It's ten o'clock now. If I come to the studio in half an hour and bring you a photo, do you think you could still get it on the air for the midnight report?'

'Sure. I'll wait for you.'

✢

He had sensed immediately, at first whiff, that the story of the *Santopadre* fishing boat was bad news. In fact, he'd done everything he could to steer clear of it. But now chance had grabbed him by the hair and ground his face in it, as one does with cats to teach them not to pee in certain places. Livia and François would have needed only to return a few moments later, and the kid would never have seen his uncle's picture on TV, the dinner would have proceeded peacefully, and everything would have gone just fine. He cursed himself for being such an incurable cop. Anyone else in his place would have said, 'Oh yeah? The kid recognized his uncle, did he? How about that!'

And he would have brought the first forkful to his mouth. But he couldn't. He had to dive in and knock his head against it. The instinct of the hunt, it was once called by Dashiell Hammett, who understood these things well.

'Where's the photo?' asked Nicolò as soon as Montalbano walked in.

It was the one of Karima and her son.

'Do you want me to frame the whole thing? Or just a detail?'

'As is.'

Nicolò Zito left the room, then soon returned without the photograph and sat himself comfortably down.

'Tell me everything. But most of all, tell me about the snack thief, which Pippo Ragonese thinks is bullshit but I don't.'

'I haven't got the time, Nicolò, believe me.'

'No, I don't believe you. Question: was the boy stealing snacks the one in the photo you just gave me?'

He was dangerously intelligent, this Nicolò. Better play along.

'Yes, that's him.'

'And who's the mother?'

'She's someone who was definitely involved in the murder the other day – you know, the guy found in the lift.

But no more questions. As soon as I manage to make some sense of this, you'll be the first to know, I promise.'

'Could you tell me at least what I'm supposed to say about the photo?'

'Right, of course. Your tone should be that of somebody telling a sad, sorrowful story.'

'So you're a director now?'

'You should say that an elderly Tunisian woman came to you in tears, begging you to show that photo on TV. She's had no news of either mother or child for three days. Their names are Karima and François. Anyone who's seen them, etcetera, anonymity guaranteed, etcetera, should call Vigàta police headquarters, etcetera.'

'Up yours, etcetera,' said Nicolò Zito.

*

Back at home, Livia went to bed immediately, taking the kid along with her. Montalbano, on the other hand, stayed up, waiting for the midnight news report. Nicolò did what he was supposed to do, keeping the photo on screen as long as possible. When the programme was over, the inspector called to thank him.

'Could you do me another favour?'

'I've half a mind to charge you a fee. What do you want?'

'Could you run the segment again tomorrow on the one p.m. news? I don't think too many people saw it at this hour.'

'Yes, sir!'

He went into the bedroom, released François from

Livia's embrace, picked the child up, took him into the living room and put him down to sleep on the sofa that Livia had already made up. He then took a shower and got into bed. Livia, though asleep, felt him beside her and nudged closer with her back to him, pressing her whole body against him. She had always liked to do it this way, half-asleep, in that pleasant no-man's-land between the country of sleep and the city of consciousness. This time, however, as soon as Montalbano began to caress her, she moved away.

'No. François might wake up.'

For a moment, Montalbano stiffened, petrified. He hadn't considered this other aspect of familial bliss.

*

He got up. Sleep, in any case, had abandoned him. On their way back to Marinella, he'd had something in mind that he wanted to do, and now he remembered what it was.

'Valente? Montalbano here. Sorry to bother you at home, especially at this hour. I need to see you at once, it's extremely urgent. Would it be all right if I came to Mazàra tomorrow morning, around ten?'

'Sure. Could you give me some—'

'It's a complicated, confusing story. I'm going purely on a hunch. It's about that Tunisian who was killed.'

'Ben Dhahab.'

'Just for starters, his name was Ahmed Moussa.'

'Holy shit.'

'Exactly.'

ELEVEN

'There's not necessarily any connection,' observed Vice-Commissioner Valente after Montalbano had finished telling his story.

'If that's your opinion, then do me a big favour. We'll keep each to his own side: you go ahead and investigate why the Tunisian used an assumed name, and I'll look for the reasons for Lapècora's murder and Karima's disappearance. And if we happen to cross paths along the way, we'll pretend we don't know each other and won't even say hello. Okay?'

'Jesus! Why don't you fly straight off the handle!'

Inspector Angelo Tomasino, a thirty-year-old with the look of a bank teller, the kind who hand counts five hundred thousand lire in small bills ten times before handing them over to you, threw down his ace, in support of his boss, 'Anyway, it's not necessarily true.'

'What's not necessarily true?'

'That Ben Dhahab is an assumed name. His full name

might have been Ben Ahmed Dhahab Moussa. Who knows, with these Arab names?'

'I won't bother you any longer,' said Montalbano, standing up.

His blood was boiling, and Valente, who had known him a long time, realized this.

'What should we do, in your opinion?' he asked simply.

The inspector sat back down.

'Find out, for example, who knew him here in Mazàra. How he managed to sign on to that fishing boat. If his papers were in order. Go and search his living quarters. Do I have to tell you to do these things?'

'No,' said Valente. 'I just like to hear you say them.'

He picked up a sheet of paper from his desk and handed it to Montalbano. It was a search warrant for the home of Ben Dhahab, complete with stamp and signature.

'This morning I woke up the judge at the crack of dawn,' Valente said, smiling. 'Care to come along for the ride?'

*

The widow Ernestina Locìcero, née Pipìa, was keen to point out that she wasn't a landlady by profession. She did own, by the grace of her dear departed, a *catojo*, that is, a little ground floor room that in its day had been a barber shop or, as they say now, a hair salon, though whatever they say, it was certainly not a salon. The gentlemen would see it soon enough, and anyway, what need was there for that whatdoyoucallit, that search warren? They had only to come and say, Signora Pipìa, this is how it is, and she wouldn't have made any trouble. The only people who make trouble are the ones who got something to hide, whereas she, well, as anyone in Mazàra could testify – anyone except for the sons of bitches and bastards – she'd always led, and continued to lead, a clean life, squeaky clean. What was the late Tunisian man like? Look, gentlemen, on no account would she ever have rented a room to an African – not to one who was black as ink nor to one whose skin din't look no different than a Mazarese's. Nothing doing. She was scared of those Africans. So why did she rent the room to Ben Dhahab? He was so well bred, gentlemen! A real man of distinction, the likes of which you don't find anymore, not even in Mazàra. Yes, sir, he spoke 'Talian, or least managed to get his point across most of the time. He even showed her his passport—

'Just a second,' said Montalbano.

'Just a minute,' said Valente at the same time.

Yessirs, his passport. All in order. Written the way the Arabs write, and there were even words written in a foreign language. Ingrish? Frinch? Dunno. The photograph matched. And if the gentlemen really, really wanted to know, she'd even filed an official rental statement, as required by law.

'When did he arrive, exactly?' Valente asked.

'Exactly ten days ago.'

And in ten days he'd had enough time to settle in, find work, and get killed.

'Did he tell you how long he planned to stay?' Montalbano asked.

'Another ten days. But . . .'

'But?'

'Well, he wanted to pay me for a whole month in
advance.'

'And how much did you ask of him?'

'I asked him straightaway for nine hundred thousand.
But you know what Arabs are like, they bargain and bargain,
and so I was ready to come down to, I dunno, six hundred, five hundred thousand . . . But the man didn't even
let me finish. He just put his hand in his pocket, pulled
out a roll of bills as fat as the belly of a bottle, took off
the rubber band holding 'em together, and counted out
nine one-hundred-thousand-lire bills.'

'Give us the key and explain a little better where this
place is,' Montalbano cut in. The Tunisian's good breeding
and distinction, in the eyes of the widow Locìcero, were
concentrated in that roll of bills as fat as the belly of a
bottle.

'Gimme a minute to get ready and I'll come with you.'

'No, signora, you stay here. We'll bring the key back
to you.'

*

A rusty iron bed, a wobbly table, an armoire with a piece
of plywood in place of the mirror, three wicker chairs. A
small bathroom with toilet and sink, and a dirty towel;
and on a shelf, a razor, a tin of shaving cream and a comb.

They went back into the single room. There was a blue canvas suitcase on a chair. They opened it: empty.

Inside the armoire, a new pair of trousers, a dark, very clean jacket, four pairs of socks, four pairs of briefs, six handkerchiefs, two undershirts: all brand new, not yet worn. In one corner of the armoire was a pair of sandals in good condition; in the opposite corner, a small plastic bag of dirty laundry. They emptied it onto the floor: nothing unusual. They stayed about an hour, searching everywhere. When they'd lost all hope, Valente got lucky. Not hidden, but clearly dropped and left wedged between the iron headboard and the bed, was a Rome-Palermo plane ticket, issued ten days earlier and made out to Mr Dhahab. So Ahmed had arrived in Palermo at ten o'clock in the morning, and two hours later, at the most, he was in Mazàra. To whom had he turned to find a place to rent?

'Did Montelusa send you the personal effects along with the body?'

'Of course,' replied Valente. 'Ten thousand lire.'

'Passport?'

'No.'

'What about all that money he had?'

'If he left it here, I'm sure the signora took care of it. The one who leads a squeaky-clean life.'

'He didn't even have his house keys in his pocket?'

'Not even. How do I have to say it? Should I sing it? He had ten thousand lire and nothing else.'

*

Summoned by Valente, Master Rahman, an elementary-school teacher who looked like a pure Sicilian and served as an unofficial liaison between his people and the Mazarese authorities, arrived in ten minutes.

Montalbano had met him the year before, when involved in the case later dubbed 'the terracotta dog'.

'Were you in the middle of a lesson?' asked Valente.

In an uncommon show of good sense, a school principal in Mazàra, without involving the superintendency, had allowed some classrooms to be used to create a school for the local Tunisian children.

'Yes, but I called in a substitute. Is there a problem?'

'Perhaps you could help clarify something for us.'

'About what?'

'About whom, rather. Ben Dhahab.'

They had decided, Valente and Montalbano, to sing only half the Mass to the schoolteacher. Afterwards, depending on his reactions, they would determine whether or not to tell him the whole story.

Upon hearing that name, Rahman made no effort to hide his uneasiness.

'What would you like to know?'

It was up to Valente to make the first move; Montalbano was only a guest.

'Did you know him?'

'He came and introduced himself to me about ten days ago. He knew who I was and what I represent. You see, last January or thereabouts, a Tunis newspaper published an article on our school.'

'And what did he say to you?'

'He said he was a journalist.'

Valente and Montalbano exchanged a very quick glance.

'He wanted to do a feature on the lives of our countrymen in Mazàra. But he intended to present himself to everyone as somebody looking for a job. He also wanted to sign on with a fishing boat. I introduced him to my colleague El Madani. And he put him in touch with Signora Pipìa about renting a room.'

'Did you ever see him again?'

'Of course. We ran into each other a few times by chance. We also were both at the same festival. He had become, well, perfectly integrated.'

'Was it you who set him up with the fishing boat?'

'No. It wasn't El Madani, either.'

'Who paid for his funeral?'

'We did. We have a small emergency fund that we set up for such things.'

'And who gave the TV reporters the photos and information on Ben Dhahab?'

'I did. You see, at that festival I mentioned, there was a photographer. Ben Dhahab objected; he said he didn't want anyone taking his picture. But the man had already taken one. And so, when the TV reporter showed up, I got hold of that photo and gave it to him, along with the bit of information Ben Dhahab had told me about himself.'

Rahman wiped away his sweat. His uneasiness had increased. And Valente, who was a good policeman, let him stew in his juices.

'But there's something strange in all this,' Rahman decided.

Montalbano and Valente seemed not even to have heard him, looking as if their minds were elsewhere. But in fact they were paying very close attention, like cats that, keeping their eyes closed as if asleep, are actually counting the stars.

'Yesterday I called the newspaper in Tunis to tell them about the incident and to make arrangements for the body. As soon as I told the editor that Ben Dhahab was dead, he started laughing and said my joke wasn't very funny: Ben Dhahab was in the room right next to his at that very moment, on the telephone. And then he hung up.'

'Couldn't it simply be a case of two men with the same name?' Valente asked provocatively.

'Absolutely not! He was very clear with me! He specifically said he'd been sent by that newspaper. He therefore lied to me.'

'Do you know if he had any relatives in Sicily?' Montalbano stepped in for the first time.

'I don't know, we never talked about that. If he'd had any in Mazàra, he certainly wouldn't have turned to me for help.'

Valente and Montalbano again consulted each other with a glance, and Montalbano, without speaking, gave his friend the go-ahead to fire the shot.

'Does the name Ahmed Moussa mean anything to you?'

It was not a shot, but an out-and-out cannon blast. Rahman jumped out of his chair, fell back down in it, then wilted.

'What . . . what . . . has . . . Ahmed Moussa got to do with this?' the schoolmaster stammered, breathless.

'Pardon my ignorance,' Valente continued implacably, 'but who is this man you find so frightening?'

'He's a terrorist. Somebody who . . . a murderer. A blood-thirsty killer. But what has he got to do with any of this?'

'We have reason to believe that Ben Dhahab was really Ahmed Moussa.'

'I feel ill,' Schoolmaster Rahman said in a feeble voice.

*

From the earth-shaken words of the devastated Rahman, they learned that Ahmed Moussa, whose real name was more often whispered than stated aloud and whose face was practically unknown, had formed a paramilitary cell of desperadoes some time before. He had introduced himself to the world three years earlier with an unequivocal calling card, blowing up a small cinema that was showing French cartoons for children. The luckiest among the audience were the ones who died; dozens of others were left blinded, maimed, or disabled for life. The cell espoused, in its communiqués at least, a nationalism so absolute as to be almost abstract. Moussa and his people were viewed with suspicion by even the most intransigent of fundamentalists. They had access to almost unlimited amounts of money, the source of which remained unknown. A large bounty had been placed on Ahmed Moussa's head by the Tunisian government. This was all that Master Rahman knew. The idea that he had somehow helped the terrorist so troubled him that he trembled and teetered as if suffering a violent attack of malaria.

'But you were deceived,' said Montalbano, trying to console him.

'If you're worried about the consequences,' Valente added, 'we can vouch for your absolute good faith.'

Rahman shook his head. He explained that it wasn't fear he was feeling, but horror. Horror at the fact that his own life, however briefly, had intersected with that of a cold-blooded killer of innocent children.

They comforted him as best they could, and as they were leaving they warned him not to repeat a word of their conversation to anyone, not even to his colleague and friend El Madani. They would call him if they needed him for anything else.

'Even at night, you call, no disturb,' said the school-teacher, who suddenly had difficulty speaking Italian.

✻

Before discussing everything they'd just learned, they ordered some coffee and drank it slowly, in silence.

'Obviously the guy didn't sign on to learn how to fish,' Valente began.

'Or to get killed.'

'We'll have to see how the captain of the fishing boat tells the story.'

'You want to summon him here?'

'Why not?'

'He'll end up repeating what he already told Augello. It might be better first to try and find out what people down on the docks think. A word here, a word there, and we might end up learning a lot more.'

'I'll put Tomasino on it.'

Montalbano grimaced. He really couldn't stand Valente's second-in-command, but this wasn't a very good reason, and it especially wasn't something he could say.

'You don't like that idea?'

'Me? It's you who have to like the idea. Your men are yours. You know them better than I do.'

'C'mon, Montalbano, don't be a shit.'

'Okay, I don't think he's right for the job. The guy acts like a tax collector, and nobody's going to feel like confiding in him when he comes knocking.'

'Yeah, you're right. I'll put Tripodi on it. He's a smart kid, fearless. And his father's a fisherman.'

'The important thing is to find out exactly what happened on the night the trawler crossed paths with the motor patrol. There's something about the whole story that doesn't add up, no matter which way you look at it.'

'And what would that be?'

'Let's forget, for the moment, how he managed to sign on with the boat. Ahmed set out with specific intentions, which are unknown to us. Here I ask myself: did he reveal these intentions to the captain and the crew? And did he reveal them before they put out or when they were already at sea? In my opinion, he did state his intentions – though I don't know exactly when – and everyone agreed to go along with him. Otherwise they would have turned around and put him ashore.'

'He could have forced them at gun point.'

'But in that case, once they put in at Vigàta or Mazàra, the captain and crew would have said what happened. They had nothing to lose.'

'Right.'

'To continue. Unless Ahmed's intention was to get killed off the shores of his native land, I can come up with only two hypotheses. The first is that he wanted to be put ashore at night, at an isolated spot along the coast, so he could steal back into his country undercover. The second is that he'd arranged some sort of meeting at sea, some secret conversation, which he absolutely had to attend in person.'

'The second seems more convincing to me.'

'Me too. And then something unexpected happened.'

'They were intercepted.'

'Right. But here that hypothesis becomes more of a stretch. Let's assume the Tunisian motor patrol doesn't know that Ahmed's aboard the fishing boat. They intercept a vessel fishing in their territorial waters, they order it to stop, the fishing vessel takes off, a machine gun is fired from the patrol boat, and purely by accident it happens to kill Ahmed Moussa. This, in any case, is the story we were told.'

This time it was Valente who grimaced.

'Unconvinced?'

'It reminds me of the Warren Commission's reconstruction of the Kennedy assassination.'

'Here's another version. In place of the man he's supposed to meet, Ahmed finds someone else, who then shoots him.'

'Or else it is in fact the man he's supposed to meet, but they have a difference of opinion, an altercation, and it ends badly, with the guy shooting him.'

'With the ship's machine gun?'

He immediately realized what he'd just said. Without even asking Valente's permission, and cursing under his breath, he grabbed the phone and asked for Jacomuzzi in Montelusa. While waiting for the connection, he asked Valente, 'In the reports you were sent, did they specify the calibre of the bullets?'

'They spoke generically of firearms.'

'Hello? Who's this?' asked Jacomuzzi at the other end of the line.

'Listen, Baudo—'

'Baudo? This is Jacomuzzi.'

'But you wish you were Pippo Baudo. Would you tell me what the fuck they used to kill that Tunisian on the fishing boat?'

'Firearms.'

'How odd! I thought he'd been suffocated with a pillow!'

'Your jokes make me puke.'

'Tell me exactly what kind of firearm.'

'A sub-machine gun, probably a Skorpion. Didn't I write that in the report?'

'No. Are you sure it wasn't the ship's machine gun?'

'Of course I'm sure. Those patrol boats, you know, are equipped with weapons that can shoot down a plane.'

'Really? Your scientific precision simply amazes me, Jacomù.'

'How do you expect me to talk to an ignoramus like you?'

✳

After Montalbano related the contents of the phone call, they sat awhile in silence. When Valente finally spoke, he said exactly what the inspector was thinking.

'Are we sure the patrol boat was Tunisian?'

✳

Since it was getting late, Valente invited the inspector to his house for lunch. But as Montalbano already had first-hand experience of the vice-commissioner's wife's ghastly cooking, he declined, saying he had to leave for Vigàta at once.

He got in his car and, after a few miles, saw a trattoria right on the beach. He stopped, got out, and sat down at a table. He did not regret it.

TWELVE

It had been hours since he last spoke to Livia. He felt guilty about this; she was probably worried about him. While waiting for them to bring him a *digestivo* of anisette (the double serving of bass was beginning to weigh on his stomach), he decided to phone her.

'Everything okay there?'

'Your phone call woke us up.'

So much for being worried about him.

'You were asleep?'

'Yes. We had a very long swim. The water was warm.'

They were living it up, without him.

'Have you eaten?' asked Livia, purely out of politeness.

'I had a sandwich. I'm on the road. I'll be back in Vigàta in an hour at the most.'

'Are you coming home?'

'No, I have to go to the office. I'll see you this evening.'

It was surely his imagination, but he thought he heard something like a sigh of relief at the other end.

✻

But it took him more than an hour to get back to Vigàta. Just outside of town, five minutes away from the office, the car suddenly decided to go on strike. There was no way to get it started again. Montalbano got out, opened the bonnet, looked at the motor. It was a purely symbolic gesture, a sort of rite of exorcism, since he didn't know a thing about cars. If someone had told him the motor consisted of a string or a twisted rubber band as on certain toy vehicles, he might well have believed it. A carabinieri squad car with two men inside passed by, then stopped and backed up. They'd had second thoughts. One was a corporal, the other a ranking officer at the wheel. The inspector had never seen them before, and they didn't know Montalbano.

'Anything we can do?' the corporal asked politely.

'Thanks. I don't understand why the engine suddenly died.'

They pulled up to the edge of the road and got out. The afternoon Vigàta–Fiacca bus stopped a short distance away, and an elderly couple got on.

'Motor looks fine to me,' was the officer's diagnosis. Then he added with a smile, 'Shall we have a look at the petrol tank?'

There wasn't a drop.

'Tell you what, Mr . . .'

'Martinez, Claudio Martinez. I'm an accountant,' said Montalbano.

No one must ever know that Inspector Montalbano was rescued by the carabinieri.

'All right, Mr Martinez, you wait here. We'll go to the nearest petrol station and bring back enough petrol to get you back to Vigàta.'

'You're very kind.'

He got back in the car, fired up a cigarette, and immediately heard an ear-splitting horn blast behind him. It was the Fiacca–Vigàta bus wanting him to get out of the way. He got out and used gestures to indicate that his car had broken down. The bus driver steered around him with a great show of effort and, once past the inspector's car, stopped at the same point where the other bus, going in the other direction, had stopped. Four people got off.

Montalbano sat there staring at the bus as it headed towards Vigàta. Then the carabinieri returned.

*

By the time he got to the office it was already four o'clock. Augello wasn't in. Fazio said he'd lost track of him since morning; Mimì'd stuck his head in at nine and then disappeared. Montalbano flew into a rage.

'Everybody does whatever they please around here! Anything goes! Ragonese will turn out to have been right, just wait and see!'

News? Nothing. Oh yes, the widow Lapècora phoned to inform the inspector that her husband's funeral would be held on Wednesday morning. And there was a land surveyor by the name of Finocchiaro who'd been waiting since two to speak to him.

'Do you know him?'

'By sight. He's retired, an old guy.'

'What's he want?'

'He wouldn't tell me. But he seems a tad upset.'

'Let him in.'

Fazio was right. The man looked shaken. The inspector asked him to sit down.

'Could I have some water, please?' asked the land surveyor, whose throat was obviously dry.

After drinking his water, he said his name was Giuseppe Finocchiaro, seventy-five years old, unmarried, former land surveyor, now retired, residing at Via Marconi 38. Clean record, not even a parking fine.

He stopped and drank the last gulp of water remaining in the glass.

'On TV today, on the afternoon news, they showed a photograph. A woman and child. You know how they said to inform you if we recognized them?'

'Yes.'

Yes. One more syllable, at that moment, might have sparked a doubt, a change of mind.

'I know the woman. Her name's Karima. The kid I've never seen before. In fact I never knew she had a son.'

'How do you know her?'

'She comes to clean my house once a week.'

'What day?'

'Tuesday mornings. She stays for four hours.'

'Tell me something. How much did you pay her?'

'Fifty thousand. But . . .'

'But?'

'Sometimes as much as two hundred thousand for extras.'

'Like blow jobs?'

The calculated brutality of the question made the surveyor first turn pale, then red.

'Yes.'

'So, let me get this straight. She would come to your house four times a month. How often did she perform these "extras"?'

'Once a month, twice at the most.'

'How did you meet her?'

'A friend of mine, retired like me, told me about her. Professor Mandrino, who lives with his daughter.'

'So no extras for the professor?'

'There were extras just the same. The daughter's a teacher, so she's out of the house every morning.'

'What day did Karima go to the professor's house?'

'On Saturday.'

'If you haven't anything else to tell me, you can go, Mr Finocchiaro.'

'Thank you for being so understanding.'

The man stood up awkwardly and eyed the inspector.

'Tomorrow is Tuesday,' he said.

'So?'

'Do you think she'll come?'

He didn't have the heart to disappoint him.

'Maybe. If she does, let me know.'

✳

Then the procession began. Preceded by his howling mother, 'Ntonio, the little boy Montalbano had met at Villaseta, who'd been punched because he wouldn't hand over his food, walked in. He'd recognized the thief in the photo they showed on TV. That was him, no doubt about it. 'Ntonio's mother, shouting loud enough to wake the dead and hurling curses and expletives, presented her demands to the horrified inspector: thirty years for the thief, life imprisonment for the mother. And in case earthly justice did not agree, from divine justice she demanded galloping consumption for the mother and a long, debilitating illness for the boy.

The son, however, unfazed by his mother's hysteria, shook his head.

'Do you also want him to die in jail?' the inspector asked him.

'No,' the boy said decisively. 'Now that I seen him calm, he looks nice.'

*

The 'extras' granted Paolo Guido Mandrino, a seventy-year-old professor of history and geography, now retired, consisted of a little bath Karima would give him. On one of the four Saturday mornings when she came, the professor would wait for her under the bedclothes, naked. When Karima ordered him to go and take his bath, Paolo Guido would pretend to be very reluctant. And so Karima, yanking down the sheets, would force the professor to turn over and would proceed to spank him. When he finally got in the bath, Karima would carefully cover him with soap and then wash him. That was all. Price of the extras: one hundred and fifty thousand lire; price of the house cleaning: fifty thousand lire.

*

'Montalbano? Listen, contrary to what I told you, I can't see you today. I have a meeting with the prefect.'

'Just say when, Mr Commissioner.'

'Well, it's really not very urgent. Anyway, after what Inspector Augello said on TV—'

'Mimì?' he yelled, as if he were singing *La Bohème*.

'Yes. Didn't you know?'

'No. I was in Mazàra.'

'He appeared on the one o'clock news. He issued a firm, blunt denial. He said Ragonese hadn't heard correctly. The man being sought wasn't a snack thief, but a sneak thief, a dangerous drug addict who went around with dirty syringes for protection in case he got caught. Augello offered apologies for the entire police department. It was very effective. I think maybe Deputy Pennacchio will calm down now.'

*

'We've already met,' said Vittorio Pandolfo, accountant, as he entered the office.

'Yes,' said Montalbano. 'What do you want?'

Rude, and he wasn't just play acting. If Pandolfo was

there to talk about Karima, it meant he'd been lying when he said he didn't know her.

'I came because on TV they showed—'

'A photograph of Karima, the woman you said you knew nothing about. Why didn't you tell me anything sooner?'

'Inspector, these are delicate matters, and sometimes one feels a little embarrassed. You see, at my age—'

'You're the Thursday-morning client?'

'Yes.'

'How much do you pay her to clean your house?'

'Fifty thousand.'

'And for extras?'

'One hundred and fifty.'

Fixed rate. Except that Pandolfo got extras twice a month. But the person being bathed, in this case, was Karima. Afterwards, the accountant would lay her down on the bed and sniff her all over. And now and then, a little lick.

'Tell me something, Mr Pandolfo. Were you, Lapècora, Mandrino and Finocchiaro her regular playmates?'

'Yes.'

'And who was it that first mentioned Karima?'

'Poor old Lapècora.'

'And what was his financial situation?'

'Awfully good. He had almost a billion lire in Treasury bonds, and he also owned his flat and office.'

*

The three afternoon clients on Tuesdays, Thursdays and Saturdays lived in Villaseta, all widowers or bachelors getting on in years. The price was the same as in Vigàta. The extra granted Martino Zaccarìa, greengrocer, consisted of having her kiss the soles of his feet; with Luigi Pignataro, retired middle-school headmaster, Karima would play blindman's buff. The headmaster would strip her naked, blindfold her, then go and hide somewhere. Karima would then look for him and find him, after which she would sit down in a chair, take him in her lap and suckle him. When Montalbano asked Calogero Pipitone, an expert agronomist, what his extras were, the man looked at him, dumbfounded.

'What do you think they were, Inspector? Me on top and her on the bottom.'

Montalbano felt like embracing him.

✤

Since on Mondays, Wednesdays and Fridays Karima was employed full-time at Lapècora's, there wouldn't be any more clients. Oddly enough, Karima rested on Sundays, not Fridays. Apparently she'd adapted to local customs. Montalbano was curious to know how much she earned per month; but since he was hopeless with numbers, he opened the door to his office and asked in a loud voice, 'Anybody got a calculator?'

'Me, Chief.'

Catarella came in and pulled a calculator not much bigger than a calling card out of his pocket.

'What do you calculate on that, Cat?'

'The days,' was his enigmatic reply.

'Come back for it in a little bit.'

'I should warrant you the machine works by *ammuttuna*.'

'What do you mean?'

Catarella mistakenly thought his superior didn't understand the last word. He stepped toward the door and called
out, 'How you say *ammuttuna* in Italian?'

'Shove,' somebody translated.

'And how am I supposed to shove this calculator?'

'Same way you shove a watch when it don't run.'

Anyway, calculating Lapècora separately, Karima earned
one million two hundred thousand lire per month as a
housekeeper, to which was added another million two
hundred thousand lire for extras. At the very least, for
full-time service, Lapècora slipped her another million
lire. Which came to three million four hundred thousand
lire monthly, tax free. Forty-four million two hundred
thousand lire annually.

Karima, from what they could gather, had been working
in the area for at least four years, so that made one hundred
and seventy-six million eight hundred thousand lire.

What about the other three hundred and twenty-four
million that was in the bank book? Where had that come
from?

The calculator had worked fine; there was no need for
ammuttuna.

✼

171

A burst of applause rang out from the other rooms. What was going on? He opened his door and discovered that the man of the hour was Mimì Augello. He started foaming at the mouth.

'Knock it off! Clowns!'

They looked at him in shock and horror. Only Fazio attempted to explain the situation.

'Maybe you don't know, Chief, but Inspector Augello—'

'I already know! The commissioner called me personally, demanding an explanation. Mr Augello, of his own initiative, without my authorization – as I made certain to emphasize to the commissioner – went on TV and spoke a pile of bullshit!'

'Uh, if I may,' Augello ventured.

'No, you may not! You told a pack of lies!'

'I did it to protect all of us here, who—'

'You can't defend yourself by lying to someone who spoke the truth!'

And he went back into his office, slamming the door behind him. Montalbano, man of ironclad morals, was in a murderous rage at the sight of Augello basking in applause.

*

'May I come in?' asked Fazio, opening the door and cautiously sticking his head inside. 'Father Jannuzzo's here and wants to talk to you.'

'Let him in.'

Don Alfio Jannuzzo, who never dressed like a priest,

was well known in Vigàta for his charitable initiatives. A tall, robust man, he was about forty years old.

'I like to cycle,' he began.

'I don't,' said Montalbano, terrified at the thought that the priest might want him to participate in some sort of charity race.

'I saw that woman's photo on television.'

The two things seemed in no way connected, and the inspector began to feel uncomfortable. Might this mean that Karima did work on Sundays after all, and that her client was none other than Don Jannuzzo?

'Last Thursday, about nine o'clock in the morning, give or take fifteen minutes, I was near Villaseta, cycling down from Montelusa to Vigàta. On the other side of the road, a car was stopped.'

'Do you remember the make?'

'Yes, it was a BMW, metallic grey in colour.'

Montalbano pricked up his ears.

'A man and a woman were inside the car. It looked like they were kissing, but when I passed right beside them, the woman broke free sort of violently, then looked at me and opened her mouth as if to say something. But the man pulled her back by force and embraced her again. I didn't like the look of it.'

'Why?'

'Because it wasn't just a lovers' quarrel. The woman's eyes, when she looked at me, were full of fear. It seemed as if she was asking for help.'

'And what did you do?'

'Nothing, because the car left almost immediately. But when I saw the photograph on television today, I knew it was the woman I'd seen in the car, I could swear to it. I'm very good with faces, Inspector, and when I see a face, even for only a second, it's forever etched in my memory.'

Fahrid, pseudo-nephew of Lapècora, and Karima.

'I'm very grateful to you, Father . . .'

The priest raised a hand to stop him.

'I haven't finished yet. I took down the number plate. As I said, I didn't like what I'd seen.'

'Do you have the number with you?'

'Of course.'

From his pocket he extracted a notebook page neatly folded in four and held it out to the inspector.

'It's written down here.'

Montalbano took it between two fingers, delicately, as one does with the wings of a butterfly.

AM 237 GW.

*

In American films, the policeman had only to tell somebody the licence-plate number, and in less than two minutes, he would know the owner's name, how many children he had, the colour of his hair, and the number of hairs on his arse.

In Italy, things were different. Once they made Montalbano wait twenty-eight days, in the course of which the owner of the vehicle (as they later wrote to him) was goat-tied and burnt to a crisp. By the time the answer arrived, it had all come to nothing.

His only choice was to turn to the commissioner, who by now had perhaps ended his meeting with the prefect.

'Montalbano here, Commissioner.'

'I just got back in the office. What is it?'

'I'm calling about that woman who was kidnapped—'

'What woman who was kidnapped?'

'You know, Karima.'

'Who's that?'

To his horror he realized he was talking to the wind. He hadn't yet said an intelligible word to the commissioner about the case.

'Mr Commissioner, I'm simply mortified—'

'Never mind. What did you want?'

'I need to have a number plate traced as quickly as possible, and I want the owner's name and address.'

'Give me the number.'

'AM 237 GW.'

'I'll have something for you by tomorrow morning.'

THIRTEEN

'I set a place for you in the kitchen. The dining-room table is being used. We've already eaten.'

He wasn't blind. He couldn't help but see that the table was covered by a giant jigsaw puzzle of the Statue of Liberty, practically life-size.

'And you know what, Salvo? It took him only two hours to solve it.'

She didn't say whom, but it was clear she was talking about François, former snack thief, now family genius.

'Did you buy it for him yourself?'

Livia dodged the question.

'Want to come down to the beach with me?'

'Right now or after I've eaten?'

'Right now.'

There was a sliver of moon shedding its light. They walked in silence. In front of a little pile of sand, Livia sighed sadly.

'You should have seen the castle he made! It was fantastic! It looked like Gaudì!'

'He'll have time to make another.'

He was determined not to give up. Like a policeman, and a jealous one at that.

'What shop did you find the puzzle in?'

'I didn't buy it myself. Mimì came round this afternoon, just for a second. The puzzle belongs to a nephew of his who—'

He turned his back to Livia, thrust his hands in his pockets, and walked away, imagining dozens of Mimì's nephews and nieces in tears, systematically despoiled of their toys by their uncle.

'Come on, Salvo, stop acting like a fool!' said Livia, running up to him.

She tried to slip her arm in his; Montalbano pulled away.

'Fuck you,' Livia said calmly, and she went back to the house.

What was he going to do now? Livia had avoided the quarrel, and he would have to get it out of his system on his own. He walked irritably along the water's edge, soaking his shoes and smoking ten cigarettes.

I'm such a fucking idiot! he said to himself at a certain point. *It's obvious that Mimì likes Livia and Livia's fond of Mimì. But, this aside, I'm only giving Mimì grist for his mill. It's clear he enjoys pissing me off. He's waging a war of attrition against me, as I do against him. I have to plan a counter-offensive.*

He went home. Livia was sitting in front of the television, which she had turned down very low in order not to wake François, who was sleeping in their bed.

'I'm sorry — seriously,' he said to her as he walked past her on his way to the kitchen.

In the oven he found a casserole of mullet and potatoes that smelled inviting. He sat down and tasted his first bite: exquisite. Livia came up behind him and stroked his hair.

'Do you like it?'

'Excellent. I must tell Adelina—'

'Adelina came this morning, saw me, said "I don' wanna disturb," turned around, and left.'

'Are you telling me you made this casserole yourself?'

'Of course.'

For an instant, but only an instant, the casserole went down the wrong way when a thought popped into his head: that she'd made it only to win forgiveness for this business with Mimì. But then the deliciousness of the dish prevailed.

*

Before sitting down beside Montalbano to watch television, Livia stopped a moment to admire the jigsaw puzzle. Now that Salvo had calmed down, she could freely talk about it.

'You should have seen how fast he put it together. It was stunning. You or I would have taken longer.'

'Or we would have got bored first.'

'But that's just it. François also thinks puzzles are boring, because they have fixed rules. Every little piece, he says, is cut so that it will fit with another. Whereas it would be more fun if there were a puzzle with many different solutions!'

'He said that?'

'Yes. And he explained it better, since I was drawing it out of him.'

'And what did he say?'

'I think I understood what he meant. He was already familiar with the Statue of Liberty and therefore when he put the head together he already knew what to do; but he was forced to do it that way because the puzzle's designer had cut out the pieces in a way that obliged the player to follow his design. Is that clear so far?'

'Clear enough.'

'It would be fun, he said, if the player could actually create his own alternative puzzle with the same pieces. Don't you think that's an extraordinary thought for so small a child?'

'They're precocious nowadays,' said Montalbano, immediately cursing himself for the banality of the expression. He'd never talked about children before, and couldn't help but resort to clichés.

*

Nicolò Zito gave a summary of the Tunisian government's official statement on the fishing-boat incident. Having conducted the necessary investigations, they had no choice but to reject the protest of the Italian government, since the Italians were powerless to prevent their own fishing boats from invading Tunisian territorial waters. That night, a Tunisian military patrol boat had sighted a trawler a few miles from Sfax. They gave the order to halt, but the fishing boat tried to flee. The patrol then fired a burst of warning from the ship's machine gun that unfortunately struck and killed a Tunisian fisherman, Ben Dhahab, whose family had already been granted substantial aid by the government in Tunis. The tragic incident should serve as a lesson.

'Have you managed to find out anything about François's mother?'

'Yeah, I have a lead, but don't get your hopes up,' replied the inspector.

'If . . . if Karima were never to come back . . . what . . . would happen to François?'

'I honestly don't know.'

'I'm going to bed,' said Livia, abruptly standing up.

Montalbano took her hand and brought it to his lips.

'Don't get too attached to him.'

*

He delicately freed François from Livia's embrace and laid him down to sleep on the sofa, which had already been made up. When he got into bed, Livia pressed her back against him, and this time did not resist his caresses. On the contrary.

'And what if the boy wakes up?' Montalbano asked at the crucial moment, still acting the swine.

'If he wakes up, I'll go and console him,' Livia said, breathing heavily.

*

At seven o'clock in the morning, he slipped softly out of bed and locked himself in the bathroom. As always, the first thing he did was look at himself in the mirror and twist up his mouth. He didn't like his own face. So why the hell was he looking at it?

He heard Livia scream sharply, rushed to the door, and opened it. Livia was in the living room; the sofa was empty.

'He's run away!' she said, trembling.

In one bound, the inspector was on the veranda. He could see him: a tiny little dot at the edge of the water, walking towards Vigàta. Dressed as he was, in only his underpants, he dashed off in pursuit. François was not running, but walking with determination. When he heard footsteps coming up behind him, he stopped in his tracks, without turning round. Montalbano, gasping for air, crouched down before him but said nothing.

The little boy wasn't crying. His eyes were staring into space, past Montalbano.

'*Je veux maman,*' he said. I want Mama.

Montalbano saw Livia approaching at a run, wearing one of his shirts; he stopped her with a single gesture, giving her to understand she should go back to the house. Livia obeyed. The inspector took the boy by the hand, and they began to walk very, very slowly. For fifteen minutes neither of them said a word. When they came to a beached boat, Montalbano sat down on the sand, François sat beside him, and the inspector put his arm around him.

'*Iu persi a me matri ch'era macari cchiù nicu di tia,*' he began, telling the child he'd lost his own mother when he was even smaller than François.

They started talking, the inspector in Sicilian and the boy in Arabic, and they understood each other perfectly.

Montalbano confided things he'd never told anyone before, not even Livia.

He told him about the nights when he used to cry his heart out, head under the pillow so that his father wouldn't hear him, and the despair he would feel every morning, knowing his mother wasn't in the kitchen to make him breakfast, or, a few years later, to make him a snack to take to school. It's an emptiness that can never be filled again; you carry it with you to the grave. The child asked him if he had the power to bring his mother back. No, replied Montalbano, nobody has that power. He had to resign himself. But you had your father, observed François, who really was intelligent, and not only because Livia said so. True, I had my father. And so, the boy asked, am I really going to end up in one of those places where they put children who have no father or mother?

'That will never happen, I promise you,' said the inspector. And he held out his hand. François shook it, looking him in the eye.

＊

When he emerged from the bathroom, all ready to go to work, he saw that François had taken the puzzle apart and was cutting the pieces into different shapes with a pair of scissors. He was trying, in his naive way, to avoid following the set pattern. All of a sudden Montalbano staggered, as if struck by an electrical charge.

'Jesus!' he whispered.

Livia looked over at him and saw him trembling, eyes popping out of his head. She became alarmed.

'My God, Salvo, what is it?'

His only answer was to pick up the boy, lift him over his head, look at him from below, put him back down, and kiss him.

'François, you're a genius!' he said.

⁂

Entering the office, he nearly slammed into Mimì Augello, who was on his way out.

'Ah, Mimì. Thanks for the puzzle.'

Mimì only gaped at him, dumbfounded.

'Fazio, on the double!'

'At your service, Chief!'

Montalbano explained to him in great detail what he was supposed to do.

'Galluzzo, in my office!'

'Yes, sir.'

He explained to him in great detail what he was supposed to do.

'Can I come in?'

It was Tortorella, pushing the door open with his foot since his hands were busy carrying a stack of papers three feet high.

'What is it?'

'Didìo's complaining.'

Didìo was the administrative manager of the Police

Commissioner's Office of Montelusa. He was nicknamed 'The Scourge of God' and 'The Wrath of God' for his punctiliousness.

'What's he complaining about?'

'Says you're behind. Says you gotta sign some papers.' And he dropped the stack of papers on the desk. 'Better take a deep breath and get started.'

*

After an hour of signing, with his hand already beginning to ache, Fazio came in.

'You're right, Chief. The Vigàta–Fiacca bus makes a stop just outside town, in the Cannatello district. And five minutes later, the bus coming from the other direction, the Fiacca–Vigàta, also stops at Cannatello.'

'So somebody could, in theory, get on the bus for Fiacca in Vigàta, get off at Cannatello, and, five minutes later, get on the Fiacca–Vigàta bus and return to town.'

'Of course.'

'Thanks, Fazio. Well done.'

'Wait a minute, Chief. I brought back the ticket man from the morning line, the Fiacca–Vigàta. His name is Lopipàro. Should I get him to come in?'

'By all means.'

Lopipàro, a reed-thin, surly man of about fifty, was keen to point out at once that he was not a ticket man, but a driver whose duties included collecting tickets. As the tickets were bought in tobacco shops, he did nothing more than collect them once the passengers had boarded the bus.

'Mr Lopìparo, everything that's said in this room must remain confidential.'

The driver/ticket man brought his right hand to his heart, as if taking a solemn oath.

'Silent as the grave,' he said.

'Mr Lopìparo—'

'Lopipàro,' he corrected, stressing the penultimate syllable.

'Mr Lopipàro, do you know Mrs Lapècora, the lady whose husband was murdered?'

'I sure do. She's got a season ticket for that line. She goes back and forth to Fiacca at least three times a week. She goes to visit her sister who's sick; she's always talking about her on the bus.'

'I'm going to ask you to make an effort to remember something.'

'I'll give it my best, since you ask.'

'Last Thursday, did you see Mrs Lapècora?'

'No need to make any effort. I certainly did see her. We even had a little run-in.'

'You quarrelled with Mrs Lapècora?'

'Yessir, I sure did! Mrs Lapècora, as everybody knows, is a little tight. She's cheap. Well, on Thursday morning she caught the six-thirty bus for Fiacca. But when we stopped at Cannatello, she got off and told Cannizzaro, the driver, that she had to go back because she'd forgotten something she was supposed to take to her sister. Cannizzaro, who told me all this that same evening, let her out.

Five minutes later, on my way to Vigàta, I stopped at Cannatello, and the lady got on my bus.'

'What did you argue about?'

'She didn't want to give me a ticket for going from Cannatello to Vigàta. She claimed she shouldn't have to use up two tickets for a little mistake. But I gotta have a ticket for every person on the bus. I couldn't just look the other way, like Mrs Lapècora wanted me to.'

'It's only right,' said Montalbano. 'But tell me something. Let's say the lady manages in half an hour to get what she forgot at home. How's she going to get to Fiacca that same morning?'

'She catches the Montelusa–Trapani bus, which stops in Vigàta at exactly seven-thirty. Which means she would arrive in Fiacca only an hour late.'

*

'Ingenious,' Fazio commented after Lopipàro had left. 'How did you figure it out?'

'The little kid, François, tipped me off when he was working on a jigsaw puzzle.'

'But why did she do it? Was she jealous of the Tunisian maid?'

'No. Mrs Lapècora's a cheapskate, as the man said. She was afraid her husband would spend everything he had on that woman. But there was something else that triggered the whole thing.'

'What was that?'

'I'll tell you later. As Catarella says, "Aravice is a nasty vice". It was greed, you see, that brought her to Lopipàro's attention, when she should have been making every effort to remain unnoticed.'

⁕

'First it took me half an hour to find out where she lived, then I wasted another half hour trying to persuade the old lady, who didn't trust me. She was afraid of me, but she calmed down when I asked her to come out of the house and she saw the police car. She made a small bundle of her things and then got in the car. You should have heard how the child cried with delight when, to his surprise, she appeared out of nowhere! They gave each other a big hug. And your lady friend was also very moved.'

'Thanks, Gallù.'

'When do you want me to come by to drive her back to Montelusa?'

'Don't worry about it, I'll take care of it.'

Their little family was growing without mercy. Now Grandma Aisha was also at Marinella.

⁕

He let the phone ring a long time, but nobody answered. The widow Lapècora wasn't home. She must certainly be out shopping. There might, however, be another explanation. He dialled the number to the Cosentino household. The security guard's likeable, moustachioed wife answered, speaking in a soft voice.

'Is your husband asleep?'

'Yes, Inspector. Do you want me to call him?'

'There's no need. You can give him my regards. Listen, signora: I tried calling Mrs Lapècora, but there was no answer. Do you know by any chance if she—'

'You won't find her in this morning, Inspector. She went to Fiacca to see her sister. She went today because tomorrow morning, at ten o'clock, she's got the funeral of the dear—'

'Thanks, signora.'

He hung up. Maybe this would simplify what needed to be done.

'Fazio!'

'At your orders, Chief.'

'Here are the keys to Lapècora's office, Salita Granet 28. Go inside and take the set of keys that are in the middle drawer of the desk. There's a little tag attached to them that says "home". It must be an extra set that he used to keep at the office. Then go to Mrs Lapècora's house and let yourself in with those keys.'

'Wait a second. What if she's there?'

'She's not. She's out of town.'

'What do you want me to do?'

'In the dining room there's a glass cupboard with dishes, cups, trays and whatnot. Take something from it, anything you like, but make sure it's something she can't deny is hers. The ideal thing would be a cup from a complete set. Then bring it here. And don't forget to put the keys back in their drawer at the office.'

'And what if the widow notices a cup is missing when she comes back?'

'We don't give a fuck. Then you must do one more thing. Phone Jacomuzzi and tell him that by the end of the day, I want the knife that was used to kill Lapècora. If he doesn't have anyone who can bring it to me, go and get it yourself.'

*

'Montalbano? This is Valente. Could you be here in Mazàra by four o'clock this afternoon?'

'If I leave immediately. Why?'

'The captain of the fishing boat is coming, and I'd like you to be there.'

'Thanks, I appreciate it. Has your man managed to find anything out?'

'Yes, and it didn't take much. He said the fishermen are quite willing to talk.'

'What did they say?'

'I'll tell you when you get here.'

'No, tell me now, so I can give it some thought on the way.'

'Okay. We're convinced the crew knew little or nothing about the whole business. They all claim the vessel was just outside our territorial waters, that it was a very dark night, and that they clearly saw a vessel approaching them on the radar screen.'

'So why did they keep going?'

'Because it didn't occur to any of the crew that it might

be a Tunisian patrol boat or whatever it was. I repeat, they were in international waters.'

'And then?'

'Then, without warning, came the signal to halt. Our fishing boat – or its crew at least, I can't speak for the captain – thought it was our Customs Police making a routine check. So they stopped, and they heard people speaking Arabic. At this point the Tunisian on the Italian boat went astern and lit a cigarette. And got shot. Only then did the fishing boat turn and flee.'

'And then?'

'And then what, Montalbà? How long is this phone call going to last?'

FOURTEEN

Unlike most men of the sea, Angelo Prestìa, crew chief and owner of the *Santopadre* motor trawler, was a fat, sweaty man. But he was sweating because it was natural for him, not because of the questions Valente was asking him. Actually, in this regard, he seemed not only calm, but even slightly put out.

'I don't understand why you suddenly wanna drag this story out again. It's water under the bridge.'

'We'd merely like to clear up a few small details, then you'll be free to go,' Valente said to reassure him.

'Well, out with it then, for God's sake!'

'You've always maintained that the Tunisian patrol boat was acting illegally, since your vessel was in international waters. Is that correct?'

'Of course it's correct. But I don't see why you're interested in questions that are the concern of the Harbour Office.'

'You'll see later.'

'But I don't need to see anything, if you don't mind!

Did the Tunisian government issue a statement or didn't they? And in this statement, did they say they killed the Tunisian themselves or didn't they? So why do you want to hash it all out again?'

'There's already a discrepancy,' Valente observed.

'Where?'

'You, for example, say the attack occurred in international waters, whereas they say you'd already crossed their border. Is that a discrepancy or isn't it, as you might say?'

'No, sir, it is not a discrepancy. It's a mistake.'

'On whose part?'

'Theirs. They obviously took their bearings wrong.'

Montalbano and Valente exchanged a lightning-quick glance, which was the signal to begin the second phase of their pre-arranged interrogation.

'Mr Prestìa, do you have a criminal record?'

'No, sir.'

'But you have been arrested.'

'You guys really have a thing for old stories, don't you! Yes, sir, I was arrested, because some poof, some sonofabitch had a grudge against me and reported me. But then the judge realized the bastard was a liar, and so he let me go.'

'What were you accused of?'

'Smuggling.'

'Cigarettes or drugs?'

'The second.'

'And your whole crew also ended up in the slammer, didn't they?'

'Yessir, but they all got out 'cause they were innocent like me.'

'Who was the judge that threw the case out of court?'

'I don't remember.'

'Was it Antonio Bellofiore?'

'Yeah, I think it was him.'

'Did you know he was thrown in jail himself a year later for rigging trials?'

'No, I didn't know. I spend more time at sea than on land.'

Another lightning-quick glance, and the ball was passed to Montalbano.

'Let's forget these old stories,' the inspector began. 'Do you belong to a co-operative?'

'Yes, the Mafico.'

'What does it stand for?'

'Mazarese Fishermen's Co-operative.'

'When you sign up a Tunisian fisherman, do you choose him yourself or is he referred to you by the co-operative?'

'The co-op tells us which ones to take,' Prestia replied, starting to sweat more than usual.

'We happen to know that the co-operative furnished you with a certain name, but you chose Ben Dhahab instead.'

'Listen, I didn't know this Ben Dhahab, never seen 'im before in my life. When he showed up on board five minutes before we put out, I thought he was the one sent by the co-op.'

'You mean Hassan Tarif?'

'I think that was 'is name.'

'Okay. Why didn't the co-operative ask you for an explanation?'

Captain Prestìa smiled, but his face was drawn and by now he was bathed in sweat.

'But this kind of stuff happens every day! They trade places all the time! The important thing is to avoid complaints.'

'So why didn't Hassan Tarif complain? After all, he lost a day's wages.'

'You're asking me? Go ask him.'

'I did,' Montalbano said calmly.

Valente looked at him in astonishment. This part had not been pre-arranged.

'And what did he tell you?' Prestìa asked almost defiantly.

'He said Ben Dhahab came to him the day before and asked if he was signed on with the *Santopadre*, and when he said yes, Dhahab told him not to show up for three days and gave him a whole week's pay.'

'I don't know anything about that.'

'Let me finish. Given this fact, Dhahab certainly didn't sign on because he needed work. He already had money. Therefore he must have come on your boat for another reason.'

Valente paid very close attention to the trap Montalbano was setting. The bit about this mysterious Tarif taking money from Dhahab had clearly been invented by the inspector, and Valente needed to know what he was driving at.

'Do you know who Ben Dhahab was?'

'A Tunisian looking for work.'

'No, my friend, he was one of the biggest names in narcotics traffic.'

While Prestìa was turning pale, Valente understood that it was now his turn. He secretly smiled to himself. He and Montalbano made a formidable duo, like Totò and Peppino.

'Looks like you're in a fix Mr Prestìa,' Valente began in a compassionate, almost fatherly tone.

'But why?'

'Come on, can't you see? A drug trafficker the calibre of Ben Dhahab signs on with your fishing boat, sparing no expense. And you have the past record you do. I, therefore, have two questions. First: what is one plus one? And second: what went wrong that night?'

'You're trying to mess me up! You want to ruin me!'

'You're doing it yourself, with your own two hands.'

'No! No! This has gone too far!' said Prestìa, very upset. 'They guaranteed me that . . .'

He stopped short, wiped off his sweat.

'Guaranteed you what?' Montalbano and Valente asked at the same time.

'That I wouldn't have any trouble.'

'Who did?'

Captain Prestìa stuck his hand in his pocket, dug out his wallet, extracted a calling card, and threw it onto Valente's desk.

*

Having disposed of Prestìa, Valente dialled the number on the calling card. It belonged to the prefecture of Trapani.

'Hello? This is Vice-Commissioner Valente from Mazàra. I'd like to speak with Commendatore Mario Spadaccia, chief of the cabinet.'

'Please hold.'

'Hello, Commissioner Valente. This is Spadaccia.'

'Sorry to disturb you, Commendatore, but I have a question concerning the killing of that Tunisian on the fishing boat—'

'Hasn't that all been cleared up? The government in Tunis—'

'Yes, I know, Commendatore, but—'

'Why are you calling me?'

'Because the crew chief of the fishing boat—'

'He gave you my name?'

'He gave us your card. He was keeping it as some sort of . . . guarantee.'

'Which indeed it was.'

'Excuse me?'

'Let me explain. You see, some time ago, His Excellency . . .' (*Wasn't that title abolished half a century ago?* Montalbano wondered while listening in on an extension.) '. . . His Excellency the prefect received an urgent request. He was asked to give his full support to a Tunisian journalist who wanted to conduct a sensitive investigation among his compatriots here, and who, for this reason, among others, also wished to sign on with one of our fishing boats. His Excellency authorized me to oversee the matter. Captain Prestìa's name was brought to my attention; I was told he was very reliable. Prestìa, however, had some worries about getting in trouble with the employment office. That's why I gave him my card. Nothing more.'

'Commendatore, I thank you very much for your thorough explanation,' said Valente. And he hung up.

They sat there in silence, eyeing each other.

'The guy's either a fuck-up or he's putting one over on us,' said Montalbano.

'This whole thing's beginning to stink,' Valente said pensively.

'Yeah,' said Montalbano.

*

They were discussing what their next move should be when the phone rang.

'I told them I wasn't here for anyone!' Valente shouted angrily. He picked up, listened a moment, then passed the receiver to Montalbano.

Before leaving for Mazàra, the inspector had left word at the office as to where he could be found if needed.

'Hello? Montalbano here. Who's this? Ah, is that you, Mr Commissioner?'

'Yes, it's me. Where have you run off to?'

He was irritated.

'I'm here with my colleague, Vice-Commissioner Valente.'

'He's not your colleague. He's a vice-commissioner and you're not.'

Montalbano started to feel worried.

'What's going on, Commissioner?'

'No, *I'm* asking *you* what the hell is going on?'

Hell? The commissioner said 'hell'?

'I don't understand.'

'What kind of crap have you been digging up?'

Crap? Did the commissioner say 'crap'? Was this the start of the Apocalypse? Would the trumpets of Judgment soon begin to sound?

'But what have I done wrong?'

'Yesterday you gave me a number plate, remember?'

'Yes. AM 237 GW.'

'That's the one. Well, I immediately asked a friend of mine in Rome to look into it, to save time, at your request, and he just called me back, very annoyed. They told him that if he wants to know the name of the car's owner, he must submit a written request specifying in detail the reasons for said request.'

'That's not a problem, Commissioner. I'll explain the whole story to you tomorrow, and you, in the request, can—'

'Montalbano, you don't understand, or perhaps you won't understand. That's a cloaked number.'

'What does that mean?'

'It means the car belongs to the secret services. Is that so hard to understand?'

That was no mere stink, what they had smelled. The air itself was turning foul.

✤

As he was telling Valente about Lapècora's murder, Karima's abduction, Fahrid and Fahrid's car, which actually belonged to the secret services, a troubling thought occurred to him. He phoned the commissioner in Montelusa.

'Excuse me, Commissioner, but when you spoke with your friend in Rome about the number plate, did you tell him what it was about?'

'How could I? I don't know the first thing about what you're doing.'

The inspector heaved a sigh of relief.

'I merely said,' the commissioner continued, 'that it involved an investigation that you, Inspector Montalbano, were conducting.'

The inspector retracted his sigh of relief.

❋

'Hello, Galluzzo? Montalbano here. I'm calling from Mazàra. I think I'm going to be here late, so, contrary to what I said, I want you to go immediately to Marinella, to my house, pick up the old Tunisian lady, and take her to Montelusa. All right? You haven't got a minute to lose.'

❋

'Hello, Livia? Listen very carefully to what I say, and do exactly what I tell you to do, without arguing. I'm in Mazàra at the moment, and I don't think they've bugged our phone yet.'

'Oh my God, what are you saying?'

'I asked you, please don't argue, don't ask questions, don't say anything. You must only listen to what I say. Very soon Galluzzo will be there. He's going to pick up the old woman and take her back with him to Montelusa. No long goodbyes, please; you can tell François he'll see her again soon. As soon as Galluzzo leaves, call my office and ask for Mimì Augello. You absolutely must find him, no matter where he is. And tell him you need to see him at once.'

'What if he's busy?'

'For you, he'll drop everything and come running. You, in the meantime, will pack François's few possessions into a small suitcase, then—'

'But what do you want—'

'Quiet, understand? Quiet. Tell Mimì that, on my orders, the kid must disappear from the face of the earth. Vanish. He should hide him somewhere safe, where he'll be all right. And don't ask where he intends to take him. Is that clear? You mustn't know where François has gone. And don't start crying, it bothers me. Listen closely. Wait for about an hour after Mimì has left with the kid, then call Fazio. Tell him, in tears – you won't have to fake it since you're crying already – tell him the kid has disappeared, maybe he ran off in search of the old lady, you don't know, but in short you want him to help you find him. In the meantime, I'll have returned. And one last thing: call Palermo airport and reserve a seat on the flight to Genoa, the one that leaves around midday tomorrow. That'll give me enough time to find someone to take you there. See you soon.'

He hung up, and his eyes met Valente's troubled gaze.
'You think they'd go that far?'
'Further.'

*

'Is the story clear to you now?' asked Montalbano.

'I think I'm beginning to understand,' replied Valente.

'Let me explain better,' said the inspector. 'All in all,
things may have gone as follows: Ahmed Moussa, for his
own reasons, has one of his men, Fahrid, set up a base of
operations. Fahrid enlists the help – whether freely offered
or not, I don't know – of Ahmed's sister, Karima, who's
been living in Sicily for a few years. Then they blackmail
a man from Vigàta named Lapècora into letting them
use his old import-export business as a front. Are you
following?'

'Perfectly.'

'Ahmed, who needs to attend an important meeting
involving weapons or political support for his movement,
comes to Italy under the protection of our secret services.
The meeting takes place at sea, but in all likelihood it's a
trap. Ahmed didn't have the slightest suspicion that our
services were double-crossing him, and that they were in
cahoots with the people in Tunis who wanted to liquidate
him. Among other things, I'm convinced that Fahrid himself
was part of the plan to do away with Ahmed. The sister,
I don't think so.'

'Why are you so afraid for the boy?'

'Because he's a witness. He could recognize Fahrid the

way he recognized his uncle on TV. And Fahrid has already killed Karima, I'm sure of it. He killed her after taking her away in a car that turns out to belong to our secret services.'

'What are we going to do?'

'You, for now, are going to sit tight. I'm going to get busy creating a diversion.'

'Good luck.'

'Good luck to you, my friend.'

*

By the time he got back to headquarters it was already evening. Fazio was there waiting for him.

'Have you found François?'

'Did you go home before coming here?' Fazio asked instead of answering.

'No. I came directly from Mazàra.'

'Chief, could we go into your office for a minute?'

Once they were inside, Fazio closed the door.

'Chief, I'm a policeman. Maybe not as good a policeman as you, but still a policeman. How did you know the kid ran away?'

'What's with you, Fazio? Livia phoned me in Mazàra and I told her to call you.'

'See, Chief, the fact is, the young lady told me she was asking me for help because she didn't know where you were.'

'Touché,' said Montalbano.

'And then, she was really and truly crying, no doubt about that. Not because the boy had run away, but for some other reason, which I don't know. So I figured out what it was you wanted me to do, and I did it.'

'And what did I want you to do?'

'To raise a ruckus, make a lot of noise. I went to all the houses in the neighbourhood and asked every person I ran into. Have you seen a little boy like so? Nobody'd seen him, but now they all know he ran away. Isn't that what you wanted?'

Montalbano felt moved. This was real friendship, Sicilian friendship, the kind based on intuition, on what was left unsaid. With a true friend, one never needs to ask, because the other understands on his own and acts accordingly.

'What should I do now?'

'Keep raising a ruckus. Call the carabinieri, call every one of their headquarters in the province, call every police station, hospital, anybody you can think of. But do it unofficially, only by phone, nothing in writing. Describe the boy, show them you're worried.'

'But are we sure they won't end up finding him, Chief?'

'Not to worry, Fazio. He's in good hands.'

*

He took a sheet of paper with the station's letterhead and typed:

TO THE MINISTRY OF TRANSPORTATION AND AUTOMOBILE
REGISTRATION:

FOR DELICATE INVESTIGATION INTO ABDUCTION AND PROBABLE

HOMICIDE OF WOMAN ANSWERING TO NAME KARIMA MOUSSA

NEED NAME OWNER AUTOMOBILE LICENCE-PLATE NUMBER

AM 237 GW. KINDLY REPLY PROMPTLY. INSPECTOR SALVO

MONTALBANO.

God only knew why, whenever he had to write a fax, he composed it as if it were a telegram. He re-read it. He'd even written out the woman's name to make the bait more appetizing. They would surely have to come out in the open now.

'Gallo!'

'Yes, sir.'

'Find the fax number for Auto Registration in Rome and send this right away. Galluzzo!'

'At your service.'

'Well?'

'I took the old lady to Montelusa. Everything's taken care of.'

'Listen, Gallù. Tell your brother-in-law to be in the general vicinity of headquarters after Lapècora's funeral tomorrow. And tell him to bring a cameraman.'

'Thanks, Chief, with all my heart.'

'Fazio!'

'I'm listening.'

'It completely slipped my mind. Did you go to Mrs Lapècora's apartment?'

'Sure did. And I took a small cup from a set of twelve. I've got it over there. You wanna see it?'

'What the hell for? Tomorrow I'll tell you what to do

with it. For now, put it in a cellophane bag. Oh, and, did Jacomuzzi send you the knife?'

'Yessirree.'

✶

He didn't have the courage to leave the office. At home the hard part awaited him. Livia's sorrow. Speaking of which, if Livia was leaving, then . . . He dialled Adelina's number.

'Adelì? Montalbano here. Listen, the young lady's leaving tomorrow morning; I need to recuperate. And you know what? I haven't eaten a thing all day.'

One had to live, no?

FIFTEEN

Livia was on the veranda, sitting on the bench, utterly still, and seemed to be looking out at the sea. She wasn't crying, but her red, puffy eyes said that she'd used up her supply of tears. The inspector sat down beside her, took one of her hands and squeezed it. To Montalbano it felt as if he'd picked up something dead; he found it almost repulsive. He let it go and lit a cigarette. Livia, he'd decided, should know as little as possible about the whole affair. But it was clear she'd given the matter some thought, and her question went right to the point.

'Do they want to harm him?'

'Actually harm him, probably not. Make him disappear for a while, yes.'

'How?'

'I don't know. Maybe by putting him in an orphanage under a false name.'

'Why?'

'Because he met some people he wasn't supposed to meet.'

Still staring at the sea, Livia thought about Montalbano's last words.

'I don't understand.'

'What don't you understand?'

'If these people François met are Tunisians, perhaps
illegal immigrants, couldn't you, as policemen—'

'They're not only Tunisian.'

Slowly, as if making a great effort, Livia turned and
faced him.

'They're not?'

'No. And I'm not saying another word.'

'I want him.'

'Who?'

'François. I want him.'

'But, Livia—'

'Shut up. I want him. No one can take him away from
me like that, you least of all. I've thought long and hard
about this, you know, these last few hours. How old are
you, Salvo?'

'Forty-four, I think.'

'Forty-four and ten months. In two months you'll be
forty-five. I've already turned thirty-three. Do you know
what that means?'

'No. What what means?'

'We've been together for six years. Every now and then
we talk about getting married, and then we drop the subject.
We both do, by mutual, tacit consent. And we don't resume
the discussion. We get along so well just the way things

are, and our laziness, our egotism, gets the better of us, always.'

'Laziness? Egotism? What are you talking about? There are objective difficulties which—'

'Which you can stick up your arse,' Livia brutally concluded.

Montalbano, disconcerted, fell silent. Only once or twice in six years had Livia ever used obscenities, and it was always in troubling, extremely tense circumstances.

'I'm sorry,' Livia said softly. 'But sometimes I just can't stand your camouflage and hypocrisy. Your cynicism is more authentic.'

Montalbano, still silent, took it all in.

'Don't try to distract me from what I want to say to you. You're very good at it; it's your job. What I want to know is: when do you think we can get married? Give me a straight answer.'

'If it was only up to me . . .'

Livia leapt to her feet.

'That's enough! I'm going to bed. I took two sleeping pills and my plane leaves Palermo at midday tomorrow. But first I want to finish what I have to say. If we ever get married, it'll be when you're fifty and I'm thirty-eight. In other words, too late to have children. And we still haven't realized that somebody, God or whoever is acting in His place, has already sent us a child, at just the right moment.'

She turned her back and went inside. Montalbano

stayed outside on the veranda, gazing at the sea, but unable to bring it into focus.

*

An hour before midnight, he made sure Livia was sleeping profoundly, then he unplugged the phone, gathered together all the loose change he could find, turned off the lights, and went out. He drove to the telephone booth in the car park of the Marinella Bar.

'Nicolò? Montalbano here. A couple of things. Tomorrow morning, around midday, send somebody along with a cameraman to the neighbourhood of police headquarters. There are some new developments.'

'Thanks. What else?'

'I was wondering, do you have a very small video camera, one that doesn't make any noise? The smaller the better.'

'You want to leave posterity a document of your prowess in bed?'

'Do you know how to use this camera?'

'Of course.'

'Then bring it to me.'

'When?'

'As soon as you've finished your midnight news report. But don't ring the doorbell when you get here, Livia's asleep.'

*

'Hello, is this the prefect of Trapani? Please excuse me for calling so late. This is Corrado Menichelli of the *Corriere della Sera*. I'm calling from Milan. We recently got wind of an extremely serious development, but before publishing our report on it, we wanted to confirm a few things with you personally, since they concern you directly.'

'Extremely serious? What is this about?'

'Is it true that pressure was put on you to accommodate a certain Tunisian journalist during his recent visit to Mazàra? I advise that you think a moment before answering, in your own interest.'

'I don't need to think for even a second!' the prefect exploded. 'What are you talking about?'

'Don't you remember? That's very odd, you know, since this all happened barely three weeks ago.'

'None of this ever happened! No pressure was ever put on me! I don't know anything about any Tunisian journalists!'

'Mr Prefect, we have proof that—'

'You can't have proof of something that never happened! Let me speak immediately to the editor-in-chief!'

Montalbano hung up. The prefect of Trapani was sincere; the head of his cabinet, on the other hand, was not.

*

'Valente? Montalbano here. I just spoke to the prefect of Trapani; I was pretending to be a reporter for the *Corriere della Sera*. He doesn't know anything. The whole thing was set up by our friend, Commendatore Spadaccia.'

'Where are you calling from?'

'Not to worry. I'm calling from a phone booth. Now here's what we should do next, providing that you agree.'

To tell him, he spent every last piece of change but one.

✤

'Mimì? Montalbano here. Were you sleeping?'

'No, I was dancing. What the fuck did you expect?'

'Are you mad at me?'

'Hell, yes! After the position you put me in!'

'Me? What position?'

'Sending me to take away the boy. Livia looked at me with hatred. I had to tear him out of her arms. It made me feel sick to my stomach.'

'Where'd you take François?'

'To Calapiàno, to my sister's.'

'Is it safe there?'

'Very safe. She and her husband have a great big house with a farm, three miles from the village, very isolated. My sister has two boys, one of them the same age as François. He'll be fine there. It took me two and a half hours to get there, and two and a half to drive back.'

'Tired, eh?'

'Very tired. I won't be in tomorrow morning.'

'All right, you won't be in, but I want you at my house, in Marinella, by nine at the latest.'

'What for?'

'To pick Livia up and drive her to Palermo airport.'

'Okay.'

'How come you're suddenly not so tired any more, eh, Mimì?'

*

Livia was now having a troubled sleep, groaning from time to time. Montalbano closed the bedroom door, sat down in the armchair, and turned on the television at very low volume. On TeleVigàta, Galluzzo's brother-in-law was saying that the Foreign Ministry in Tunis had issued a statement regarding some erroneous information about the unfortunate killing of a Tunisian fisherman aboard an Italian motor trawler that had entered Tunisian waters. The statement denied the wild rumours according to which the fisherman was not, in fact, a fisherman, but the rather well-known journalist Ben Dhahab. It was an obvious case of two men with the same name, since Ben Dhahab the journalist was alive and well and still working. In the city of Tunis alone, the statement went on to say, there are more than twenty men named Ben Dhahab. Montalbano turned off the television. So the tide had started to turn, and people were running for cover, raising fences, putting up smokescreens.

*

He heard a car pull up and stop in the clearing in front of the house. The inspector rushed to the door to open up. It was Nicolò.

'I got here as fast as I could,' he said, entering.

'Thanks.'

'Livia's asleep?' the newsman asked, looking around.

'Yes. She's leaving for Genoa tomorrow morning.'

'I'm so sorry I won't have a chance to say goodbye to her.'

'Nicolò, did you bring the video camera?'

The newsman reached into his jacket pocket and pulled out a gadget no larger than four packets of cigarettes stacked two by two.

'Here you are. I'm going home to bed.'

'No you're not. First you have to hide this somewhere it won't be visible.'

'How am I going to do that, if Livia's sleeping in the next room?'

'Nicolò, I don't know why you've got it into your head that I want to film myself fucking. I want you to set up the camera in this room.'

'Tell me what it is you want to film.'

'A conversation between me and a man sitting exactly where you are now.'

Nicolò looked straight ahead and smiled.

'Those shelves full of books seem like they were put there for that very purpose.'

Taking a chair from the table, he set it next to the bookcase and climbed up on it. He shuffled a few books, set up the camera, sat back down where he was before, and looked up.

'From here you can't see it,' he said, satisfied. 'Come and check for yourself.'

The inspector checked.

'That seems fine.'

'Stay there,' said Nicolò.

He climbed back up on the chair, fussed about, and got back down.

'What's it doing?' asked Montalbano.

'Filming you.'

'Really? It makes no noise at all.'

'I told you the thing's amazing.'

Nicolò repeated his rigmarole of climbing onto the chair and stepping back down. But this time he had the camera in his hand and showed it to Montalbano.

'Here's how you do it, Salvo. To rewind the tape, you press this button. Now bring the camera up to your eye and press this other button. Go ahead, try.'

Montalbano did as he was told and saw a very tiny image of himself ask in a microscopic voice: 'What's it doing?' Then he heard Nicolò's voice say, 'Filming you.'

'Fantastic,' the inspector said. 'There's one thing, though. Is that the only way to see what you've filmed?'

'Of course not,' Nicolò replied, taking out a normal-looking video cassette that was made differently inside. 'Watch what I do. I remove the tape from the video camera, which as you can see is as small as the one in your answering machine, and I slip it inside this one, which is made for this purpose and can be used in your VCR.'

'Listen, to make it record, what do I do?'

'Push this other button.'

Seeing the inspector's expression, which looked more confused than convinced, Nicolò grew doubtful.

'Will you be able to use it?'

'Come on!' replied Montalbano, offended.

'Then why are you making that face?'

'Because I can't very well climb onto a chair in front of the man I want to film. It would make him suspicious.'

'See if you can reach it by standing on tiptoe.'

He could.

'Then it's simple. Just leave a book out on the table, then casually put it back on the shelf, meanwhile pressing the button.'

✻

Dear Livia,

Unfortunately I can't wait for you to wake up. I have to go to Montelusa to see the commissioner. I've already arranged to have Mimì come to take you to the airport. Please try to be as calm and untroubled as possible. I'll phone you this evening. Kisses,

Salvo

A travelling salesman of the lowest rank would have expressed himself with more affection and imagination. He rewrote the note and, strangely, it came out exactly the same as the previous one. Nothing doing. It wasn't true that he had to see the commissioner; he merely wanted to skip the goodbyes. It was therefore a big fat lie, and he had never been able to tell one directly to someone he respected. Little fibs, on the other hand, he was very good at. And how.

✻

At headquarters he found Fazio waiting for him, upset.

'I've been trying to call you at home for the last half hour. You must've unplugged the telephone.'

'What's the problem?'

'Some bloke phoned saying he accidentally found the dead body of an old woman in Villaseta, on Via Garibaldi, in the same house where we caught the little boy. That's why I was looking for you.'

Montalbano felt something like an electric shock.

'Tortorella and Galluzzo have already gone there. Galluzzo just phoned and said it was the same old lady he took to your house.'

Aisha.

The punch Montalbano gave himself in the face wasn't hard enough to knock out his teeth, but it made his lip bleed.

'What the hell are you doing, Chief?' said Fazio, flabbergasted.

Aisha was a witness, of course, just like François. But the inspector's eyes and attention had all been on the boy. A fucking idiot, that's what he was. Fazio handed him a handkerchief.

'Here, clean yourself up.'

✲

Aisha was a twisted little bundle at the foot of the stairs that led up to Karima's room.

'She apparently fell and broke her neck,' said Dr Pasquano, who'd been summoned by Tortorella. 'But I'll be able to tell you more after the autopsy. Although to send an old lady like this flying, you'd only need to blow on her.'

'And where's Galluzzo?' Montalbano asked Tortorella.

'He went to Montelusa to talk to a Tunisian woman the deceased was staying with. He wanted to ask her why the old lady came back here, to find out if anybody had telephoned her.'

As the ambulance was leaving, the inspector went inside Aisha's house, lifted a stone next to the fireplace, took out the bank book, blew the dust off, and put it in his pocket.

'Chief!'

It was Galluzzo. No, nobody had phoned Aisha. She'd simply decided to go home. She woke up one morning, took the bus, and did not miss her appointment with death.

*

Back in Vigàta, before going to headquarters, he stopped in at the office of a notary named Cosentino, whom he liked.

'What can I do for you, Inspector?'

Montalbano pulled out the bank book and handed it to the notary, who opened it, glanced at it, and asked, 'So?'

The inspector launched into an extremely complicated explanation; he wanted him to know only half the story.

'What I think you're saying,' the notary summarized, 'is that this money belongs to a woman you presume to be dead, and that her son, a minor, is her only heir.'

'Right.'

'And you'd like for this money to be tied up in some

way, so that the child could only enter into possession when he comes of age.'

'Right.'

'But why don't you simply hold on to the booklet yourself, and when the time comes, turn it over to him?'

'What makes you think I'll still be alive in fifteen years?'

'I see,' said the notary. He continued, 'Let's do this: you take the book back with you, I'll give the matter some thought, and let's talk again in a week. It might be a good idea to invest that money.'

'It's up to you,' said Montalbano, standing up.

'Take the book back.'

'You keep it. I might lose it.'

'Then wait and I'll give you a receipt.'

'If you'd be so kind.'

'One more thing.'

'Tell me.'

'You must be absolutely certain, you know, that the mother is dead.'

∗

From headquarters, he phoned home. Livia was about to leave. She gave him a rather chilly goodbye, or so it seemed to him. He didn't know what to do about it.

'Is Mimì there yet?'

'Of course. He's waiting in the car.'

'Have a good trip. I'll call you tonight.'

He had to move on, not let Livia tie him up.

'Fazio!'

'At your command.'

'Go to the church where Lapècora's funeral is being held. It must've already started by now. Bring Gallo along. When people are expressing their condolences to the widow, I want you to approach her and, with the darkest look you can muster up, say: 'Signora, please come with us to police headquarters.' If she starts to make a scene, starts screaming and shouting, don't hesitate to use force to put her in the squad car. And one more thing: Lapècora's son is sure to be there in the cemetery. If he tries to defend his mother, handcuff him.'

*

MINISTRY OF TRANSPORTATION AND AUTOMOBILE REGISTRATION: CONCERNING THE EXTREMELY SENSITIVE INVESTIGATION OF HOMICIDE OF TWO WOMEN NAMES KARIMA AND AISHA ABSOLUTELY MUST KNOW PERSONAL PARTICULARS AND ADDRESS OF OWNER OF AUTOMOBILE NUMBER PLATE AM 237 GW STOP PLEASE REPLY PROMPTLY STOP SIGNED SALVO MONTALBANO VIGATA POLICE MONTELUSA PROVINCE.

At the Automobile Registration office, before passing the fax on to the person in charge, they were sure to have a laugh at his expense and think him some kind of idiot for the way he formulated his request. But the person in charge, for his part, would understand the gambit, the challenge hidden in the message, and be forced to make a counter-move. Which was exactly what Montalbano wanted.

SIXTEEN

Montalbano's office was located at the opposite end of the building from the entrance to police headquarters, and yet he still heard all the shouting that broke out when Fazio's car arrived with the widow Lapècora inside. Though there were hardly any journalists or photographers around, dozens of idlers and rubberneckers must have joined their modest number.

'Signora, why were you arrested?'

'Look over here, signora!'

'Out of the way! Out of the way!'

Then there was relative calm and someone knocked at his door. It was Fazio.

'How'd it go?'

'She didn't put up much resistance. But she got upset when she saw the journalists.'

'What about the son?'

'There was a man standing next to her in the cemetery, and everyone was expressing their condolences to him too, so I thought he must be the son. But when I told the widow she had to come with us, he turned his back and walked away. So I guess he wasn't her son.'

'Ah, but he was, Fazio. Too sensitive to witness his mother's arrest. And terrified that he might have to pay her legal fees. Bring the lady in here.'

'Like a thief, that's how you're treating me! Just like a thief!' the widow burst out as soon as she saw the inspector.

Montalbano made a dark face.

'Did you mistreat the lady?'

As if reading from a script, Fazio pretended to be embarrassed.

'Well, since we were arresting her—'

'Who ever said you were arresting her? Please sit down, signora, I apologize for the unpleasant misunderstanding. I won't keep you but a few minutes, only as long as it takes to draw up a report of your answers to a few questions. Then you can go home and that'll be the end of it.'

Fazio went and sat down at the typewriter, while Montalbano sat behind his desk. The widow seemed to have calmed down a little, although the inspector could see her nerves jumping under her skin like fleas on a stray dog.

'Signora, please correct me if I'm wrong. You told me, as you'll remember, that on the morning of your husband's murder, you got out of bed, went into the bathroom, got dressed, took your bag from the dining room, and went out. Is that right?'

'Absolutely.'

'You didn't notice anything abnormal in your apartment?'

'What was I supposed to notice?'

'For example, that the door to the study, contrary to custom, was closed?'

He'd taken a wild guess, but was right on the mark. Initially red, the woman's face blanched. But her voice remained steady.

'I think it was open, since my husband never closed it.'

'No, it was not, signora. When I entered your home with you, upon your return from Fiacca, the door was closed. I reopened it myself.'

'What does it matter if it was open or closed?'

'You're right, it's a meaningless detail.'

The widow couldn't help heaving a long sigh.

'Signora, the morning your husband was murdered, you left for Fiacca to visit your ailing sister. Right?'

'That's what I did.'

'But you forgot something, and for that reason, at the Cannatello junction, you got off the bus, waited for the next bus coming from the opposite direction, and returned to Vigàta. What did you forget?'

The widow smiled; apparently she'd prepared herself for such a question.

'I did not get off at Cannatello that morning.'

'Signora, I have statements from the two bus drivers.'

'They're right, except for one thing. It wasn't that morning, but two mornings before. The bus drivers got their days wrong.'

She was shrewd and quick. He would have to resort to trickery.

He opened a drawer to his desk and took out the kitchen knife in its cellophane bag.

'This, signora, is the knife that was used to murder your husband. With only one stab wound, in the back.'

The widow's expression didn't change. She didn't say a word.

'Have you ever seen it before?'

'You see so many knives like that.'

Very slowly, the inspector again slipped his hand into the drawer, and this time he withdrew another cellophane bag, this one with a small cup inside.

'Do you recognize this?'

'Did you take that yourselves? You made me turn the house upside down looking for it!'

'So it's yours. You officially recognize it.'

'Of course I do. What use could you have for that cup?'

'It's going to help me send you to jail.'

Of all the possible reactions, the widow chose one that, in a way, won the inspector's admiration. In fact, she turned her head towards Fazio and politely, as if paying a courtesy call, asked him, 'Has he gone crazy?'

Fazio, in all sincerity, would have liked to answer that in his opinion the inspector had been crazy since birth, but he said nothing and merely stared out of the window.

'Now I'll tell you how things went,' said Montalbano. 'That morning, hearing the alarm clock, you got up and went into the bathroom. You necessarily passed by the door to the study, which you noticed was closed. At first you thought nothing of it, then you reconsidered. And when you came out of the bathroom, you opened it. But you didn't go in, at least I don't think you did. You waited a moment in the doorway, reclosed the door, went into the kitchen, grabbed the knife, and put it in your bag. Then you went out, you caught the bus, you got off at Cannatello, you got on the bus to Vigàta, you went back home, you opened the door, you saw your husband ready to go out, you argued with him, he opened the door to the lift, which was on your floor because you'd just used it. You followed behind him, you stabbed him in the back, he turned halfway around, fell to the ground, you started the lift, you reached the ground floor, and you got out. And nobody saw you. That was your great stroke of luck.'

'But why would I have done it?' the woman asked calmly. And then, with an irony that seemed incredible at that moment and in that place, 'Just because my husband had closed the door to his study?'

Montalbano, from a seated position, bowed admiringly to her.

'No, signora; because of what was behind that closed door.'

'And what was that?'

'Karima, your husband's mistress.'

'But you said yourself that I didn't go into the room.'

'You didn't need to, because you were assailed by a cloud of perfume, the very stuff that Karima wore in abundance. It's called Volupté. It has a strong, persistent scent. You'd probably smelled it before from time to time on your husband's clothes. It was still there in the study, less strong of course, when I went in that evening, after you came home.'

The widow Lapècora remained silent; she was thinking over what the inspector had just said.

'Would you answer me one question?' she then asked.

'As many as you like.'

'Why, in your opinion, didn't I go into the study and kill that woman first?'

'Because your brain is as precise as a Swiss watch and as fast as a computer. Karima, seeing you open the door, would have put herself on the defensive, ready for anything. Your husband, hearing her scream, would have come running and disarmed you with Karima's help. Whereas by pretending not to notice anything, you could wait and catch him in the act a little later.'

'And how do you explain, just to follow your argument, that my husband was the only one killed?'

'When you returned, Karima was already gone.'

'Excuse me, but since you weren't there, who told you this story?'

'Your fingerprints on the cup and on the knife told me.'

'Not on the knife!' the woman snapped.

'Why not on the knife?'

The woman started biting her lip.

'The cup is mine, the knife isn't.'

'The knife is also yours; it's got one of your fingerprints on it. Clear as day.'

'But that can't be!'

Fazio did not take his eyes off his superior. He knew there were no fingerprints on the knife. This was the most delicate moment of the trick.

'And you're so sure there are no fingerprints on the knife because when you stabbed your husband you were still wearing the gloves you'd put on when you got all dressed up to go out. You see, the fingerprint we took from it was not from that morning, but from the day before, when, after using the knife to clean the fish you had for dinner, you washed it and put it back in the kitchen drawer. In fact, the fingerprint is not on the handle, but on the blade, right where the blade and the handle meet. And now you're going to go into the next room with Fazio, and we're going to take your fingerprints and compare them.'

'He was a son of a bitch,' said Signora Lapècora, 'and he deserved to die the way he did. He brought that whore into my home to get his jollies in my bed all day while I was out.'

'Are you saying you acted out of jealousy?'

'Why else?'

'But hadn't you already received three anonymous letters? You could have caught them in the act at the office on Salita Granet.'

'I don't do that kind of thing. But when I realized he'd brought that whore into my home, my blood started to boil.'

'I think, signora, your blood started to boil a few days before that.'

'When?'

'When you discovered your husband had withdrawn a large sum from his bank account.'

This time, too, the inspector was bluffing. It worked.

'Two hundred million lire!' the widow said in rage and despair. 'Two hundred million for that disgusting whore!'

That explained part of the money in Karima's bank book.

'If I didn't stop him, he was liable to eat up the office, our home and our savings!'

'Shall we put this all in a statement, signora? But first tell me one thing. What did your husband say when you appeared before him?'

'He said: "Get the hell out of my way. I have to go to the office." He'd probably had a spat with the slut, she'd left, and he was running after her.'

*

'Mr Commissioner? Montalbano here. I'm calling to let you know that I've just now managed to get Mrs Lapècora to confess to her husband's murder.'

'Congratulations. Why did she do it?'

'Self-interest, which she's trying to disguise as jealousy. I need to ask a favour of you. Could I hold a press conference?'

There was no answer.

'Commissioner? I asked if I could—'

'I heard you perfectly well, Montalbano. It's just that I was speechless with amazement. *You* want to hold a press conference? I don't believe it!'

227

'And yet it's true.'

'All right, go ahead. But later you must explain to me what's behind it.'

*

'Are you saying that Mrs Lapècora had long known about her husband's relations with Karima?' asked Galluzzo's brother-in-law in his capacity as a reporter for TeleVigàta.

'Yes. Thanks to no less than three anonymous letters that her husband had sent to her.'

At first they didn't understand.

'Do you mean to say that Mr Lapècora actually denounced himself to his wife?' asked a bewildered journalist.

'Yes. Because Karima had started blackmailing him. He was hoping his wife's reaction would free him from his predicament. But Mrs Lapècora did not intervene. Nor did their son.'

'Excuse me, but why didn't he turn to the police?'

'Because he thought it would create a big scandal. Whereas, with his wife's help, he was hoping matters would stay within the, uh, family circle.'

'But where is this Karima now?'

'We don't know. She escaped with her son, a little boy. Actually one of her friends, who was worried about their disappearance, asked the Free Channel to air a photo of the mother and her son. But so far nobody has come forward.'

They thanked him and left. Montalbano smiled in

satisfaction. The first puzzle had been solved, perfectly, within its specific outline. Fahrid, Ahmed and even Aisha had been left out of it. With them in it, had they been properly used, the puzzle's design would have been entirely different.

*

He was early for his appointment with Valente. He stopped in front of the restaurant where he'd gone the last time he was in Mazàra. He gobbled up a sauté of clams in bread-crumbs, a heaped dish of spaghetti with white clam sauce, a roast turbot with oregano and caramelized lemon, and he topped it all off with a bitter chocolate timbale in orange sauce. When it was all over he stood up, went into the kitchen, and shook the chef's hand without saying a word, deeply moved. In the car, on his way to Valente's office, he sang at the top of his lungs: 'Guarda come dondolo, guarda come dondolo, col twist . . .'

*

Valente showed Montalbano into a room next to his own.

'It's something we've done before,' he said. 'We leave the door ajar, and you, by manipulating this little mirror, can see what's happening in my office, if hearing's not enough.'

'Be careful, Valente. It's a matter of seconds.'

'Leave it to us.'

*

Commendatore Spadaccia walked into Valente's office. It was immediately clear he was nervous.

'I'm sorry, Commissioner Valente, I don't understand. You could have easily come to the prefecture yourself and saved me some time. I'm a very busy man, you know.'

'Please forgive me, Commendatore,' Valente said with abject humility. 'You're absolutely right. But we'll make up for that at once; I won't keep you more than five minutes. I just need a simple clarification.'

'All right.'

'The last time we met, you told me the prefect had been asked in some way—'

The commendatore raised an imperious hand, and Valente immediately fell silent.

'If that's what I said, I was wrong. His Excellency knows nothing about all this. Anyway, it's the sort of bullshit we see every day. The ministry, in Rome, phoned me; they don't bother His Excellency with this kind of crap.'

Obviously the prefect, after getting the phone call from the bogus *Corriere* reporter, had asked the chief of his cabinet for an explanation. And it must have been a rather lively discussion, the echoes of which could still be heard in the strong words the commendatore was using.

'Go on,' Spadaccia urged.

Valente threw up his hands, a halo hovering over his head.

'That's all,' he said.

Spadaccia, dumbstruck, looked all around as if to verify the reality of what was happening.

'Are you telling me you have nothing more to ask me?'

'That's right.'

Spadaccia slammed his hand down on the desk with such force that even Montalbano jumped in the next room.

'You think you've made an idiot of me, but you'll pay for this, just wait and see!'

He stormed out, fuming. Montalbano ran to the window, nerves taut. He saw the commendatore shoot out of the front door like a bullet towards his car, whose driver was getting out to open the door for him. At that exact moment, the door of a squad car that had just pulled up opened, and out came Angelo Prestìa, who was immediately taken by the arm by a policeman. Spadaccia and the captain of the fishing boat stood almost face to face. They said nothing to each other, and each continued on his way.

The whinny of joy that Montalbano let out now and then when things went right for him terrified Valente, who came running from the next room.

'What's the matter with you?'

'It worked!'

'Sit down here,' they heard a policeman say. Prestìa had been brought into the office.

Valente and Montalbano stayed where they were; each lit a cigarette and smoked it without saying a word to the other. Meanwhile the captain of the *Santopadre* simmered on a low flame.

✻

They entered with faces like the bearers of black clouds and bitter cargoes. Valente went and sat behind his desk; Montalbano pulled up a chair and sat down beside him.

'When's this aggravation gonna end?' the captain began.

He didn't realize that with his aggressive attitude, he had just revealed what he was thinking to Valente and Montalbano: that is, he believed that Commendator Spadaccia had come to vouch for the truth of his testimony. He felt at peace, and could therefore be indignant.

On the desk was a voluminous folder on which Angelo Prestìa's name was written in large block letters – voluminous because it was filled with old memos, but the captain didn't know this. Valente opened it and took out Spadaccia's calling card.

'You gave this to us, correct?'

Valente's switch from the politeness of last time to a more police-like bluntness worried Prestìa.

'Of course it's correct. The commendatore gave it to me and said if I had any trouble after taking the Tunisian aboard I could turn to him. Which I did.'

'Wrong,' said Montalbano, fresh as a spring chicken.

'But that's what he told me to do!'

'Of course that's what he told you to do, but as soon as you smelled a rat, you gave that calling card to us instead. And in doing so, you put that good man in a pickle.'

'A pickle? What kind of pickle?'

'Don't you think being implicated in premeditated murder is a pretty nasty pickle?'

Prestìa shut up.

'My colleague Montalbano,' Valente cut in, 'is trying to explain to you why things went as they did.'

'And how did they go?'

'They went as follows: if you had gone directly to Spadaccia and hadn't given us his card, he would have taken care of everything, under the table, of course. Whereas you, by giving us the card, got the law involved. So that left Spadaccia with only one option: deny everything.'

'What?!'

'Yessirree. Spadaccia's never seen you before, never heard your name. He made a sworn statement, which we've added to our file.'

'The son of a bitch!' said Prestìa. Then he asked, 'And how did he explain how I got his card?'

Montalbano laughed heartily to himself.

'He fooled you there, too, pal,' he said. 'He brought us a photocopy of a declaration he made about ten days ago to the Trapani police. Says his wallet was stolen with everything inside, including four or five calling cards, he couldn't remember exactly how many.'

'He tossed you overboard,' said Valente.

'Where the water's way over your head,' Montalbano added.

'How long are you going to manage to stay afloat?' Valente piled it on.

The sweat under Prestìa's armpits formed great big blotches. The office was filled with an unpleasant odour of musk and garlic, which Montalbano saw as rot-green in colour. Prestìa put his head in his hands and muttered:

'They didn't give me any choice.'

He remained awhile in that position, then apparently made up his mind, 'Can I speak with a solicitor?'

'A solicitor?' said Valente, as if greatly surprised.

'Why do you want a solicitor?' Montalbano asked in turn. 'I thought—'

'You thought what?'

'That we were going to arrest you?'

The duo worked perfectly together.

'You're not going to arrest me?'

'Of course not.'

'You can go now, if you like.'

It took Prestìa five minutes before he could get his arse unstuck from the chair and run out the door, literally.

*

'So, what happens next?' asked Valente, who knew they had unleashed a pack of demons.

'What happens next is that Prestìa will go and pester Spadaccia. And the next move will be theirs.'

Valente looked worried.

'What's wrong?' asked Montalbano.

'I don't know . . . I'm not convinced . . . I'm afraid they'll silence Prestìa. And we would be responsible.'

'Prestìa's too visible at this point. Bumping him off would be like putting their signature on the entire operation. No, I'm convinced they *will* silence him, but by paying him off handsomely.'

'Will you explain something for me?'

'Sure.'

'Why are you stepping into this quicksand?'

'And why are you following behind me?'

'First of all, because I'm a policeman, like you, and secondly, because I'm having fun.'

'And my answer is: my first reason is the same as yours. And my second is that I'm doing it for money.'

'And what'll you gain from it?'

'I know exactly what my gain will be. But you want to bet that you'll gain something from it too?'

*

Deciding not to give in to the temptation, he sped past the restaurant where he'd stuffed himself at lunch, doing 120 kilometres an hour. A half kilometre later, however, his resolution suddenly foundered, and he slammed on the brakes, provoking a furious blast of the horn from the car behind him. The man at the wheel, while passing him, glared at him angrily and gave him the finger. Montalbano then made a U-turn, strictly prohibited on that stretch of road, went straight into the kitchen, and, without even saying hello, asked the cook, 'So, exactly how do you prepare your striped mullet?'

SEVENTEEN

The following morning, at eight o'clock sharp, he appeared at the commissioner's office. His boss, as usual, had been there since seven, amid the muttered curses of the cleaning women who felt he prevented them from doing their jobs.

Montalbano told him about Mrs Lapècora's confession, explaining how the poor murder victim, as if trying to sidestep his tragic end, had written anonymously to his wife and openly to his son, but both had let him stew in his own juices. He made no mention of either Fahrid or Moussa — of the larger puzzle, in other words. He didn't want the commissioner, now at the end of his career, to find himself implicated in an affair that stank worse than a pile of shit.

And up to this point it had gone well for him; he hadn't had to pull any wool over the commissioner's eyes. He'd only left a few things out, told a few half-truths.

'But why did you want to hold a press conference, you who usually avoid them like the plague?'

He had anticipated this question, and the answer he

had ready on his lips allowed him another at least partial omission, if not an outright lie.

'This Karima, you see, was a rather unusual sort of prostitute. She went not only with Lapècora, but with other people as well. All well on in years: retirees, businessmen, professors. By limiting the case to Lapècora, I've tried to prevent the poison, the insinuations, from spreading to a bunch of poor wretches who, in the end, didn't really do anything wrong.'

He was convinced it was a plausible explanation. And in fact, the commissioner's only comment was, 'You have strange morals, Montalbano.' And then he asked, 'But has this Karima really disappeared?'

'Apparently, yes. When she learned her lover had been killed, she ran away with her little boy, fearing she might be implicated in the homicide.'

'Listen,' said the commissioner. 'What was that business with the car all about?'

'What car?'

'Come on, Montalbano. The car that turned out to belong to the secret services. They're nasty people, you know.'

Montalbano laughed. He'd practised the laugh the night before, in front of a mirror, persisting until he got it right. Now, however, contrary to his hopes, it rang false, too high-pitched. But if he wanted to keep his excellent superior out of this mess, he no longer had any choice. He had to tell a lie.

'Why do you laugh?' asked the commissioner, surprised.

'Out of embarrassment, believe me. The person who gave me that licence number phoned me the next day and said he'd made a mistake. The letters were right, but he'd got the number wrong. It was 837, not 237. I apologize. I feel mortified.'

The commissioner looked him in the eye for what seemed like an eternity. Then he spoke in a soft voice.

'If you want me to swallow that, I'll swallow it. But be very careful, Montalbano. Those people don't mess about. They're capable of anything, and whenever they slip up, they blame it on certain colleagues who went astray. Who don't exist. They're the ones who go astray. It's in their nature.'

Montalbano didn't know what to say. The commissioner changed subject.

'Tonight you'll have dinner at my house. I don't want to hear any arguments. You'll eat whatever there is. I've got two things I absolutely have to tell you. But I won't say them here, in my office, because that would give them a bureaucratic flavour, which I find unpleasant.'

It was a beautiful day, not a cloud in the sky, and yet Montalbano had the impression that a shadow had fallen across the sun, making the room turn suddenly cold.

*

There was a letter addressed to him on the desk in his office. He checked the postmark, as he always did, to try and discover its provenance, but it was illegible. He opened the envelope and read:

Inspector Montalbano,

You dont know me and I dont know what your like. My name is Arcangelo Prestifilippo and I am your fathers business partner in the vineyard which is producing very well, thank the Lord. Your father never talks about you but I found out he collects all the newspapers that talk about you and when he sees you on tv sometimes he starts crying but tries to not let other people see.

Dear Inspector, I feel my heart give out because the news I got to tell you isnt good. Ever since Signora Giulia, your father's second wife went up to Heaven four years ago, my partner and friend hasnt been the same. Then last year he started feeling bad, he would run out of breath even just from climbing some stairs and he would get dizzy. He didnt want to go to the doctor, nothing doing. And so I took advantage because my son who works in Milan and is a good doctor, came to town, and I took him to your father's house. My son looked at him and got upset because he wanted your father to go to the hospital. He made such a big fuss and talked so much that he convinced your father to go to the hospital with him before he went back to Milan. I went to see him every night and ten days later the doctor told me they did all the tests and your father had that terrible lung disease. And so your father started going in and out of the hospital for treatment which made all his hair fall out but didnt make him one bit better. And he told me specially to not tell you about it, he said he didnt want you getting all worried. But last night I talked to the doctor and he said your father is near the end now, he got only one month maybe, give or take a few days. And so in spiter your dad's strict orders I wanted you to know whats happening. Your fathers in the Clinica Porticelli, the telefone number is 341234. Theres a phone in his room. But its better if you come and see him in person and pretend you dont know nuthin bout him being sick. You already got my phone number, its the same as the vineyard office where I work all day long.

I am very sorry.

   Best regards,
   Arcangelo Prestifilippo

A slight tremor in his hands made him struggle to put the letter back in the envelope, and so he slipped it into his pocket. A profound weariness came over him, forcing him to lean heavily, eyes closed, against the back of his chair. He had trouble breathing; there seemed suddenly to be no air in the room. He stood up with difficulty, then went into Augello's office.

'What's wrong?' asked Mimì as soon as he saw his face.

'Nothing. Listen, I've got some work to do. I mean, I need a little time alone, some peace and quiet.'

'Anything I can do to help?'

'Yes. Take care of everything yourself. I'll see you tomorrow. Don't let anybody phone me at home.'

*

He passed by the *càlia e simenza* shop, bought a sizable cornet, and began his stroll along the jetty. A thousand thoughts raced through his head, but he was unable to seize a single one. When he arrived at the lighthouse he kept on walking. Directly below the lighthouse was a large rock, slippery with green moss. In danger of falling into the sea with each step, he managed to reach the rock and sat down, cornet in hand. But he didn't open it. He felt a kind of wave surge up from some part of his lower body, ascend towards his chest, and from there continue rising towards his throat, forming a knot that took his breath away. He felt the need to cry, but the tears wouldn't come. Then, amid the jumble of thoughts crowding his brain, a few words forced their way into clarity until they came together in a line of verse:

Father, you die a little more each day . . .

What was it? A poem? By whom? And when had he read it? He repeated the line under his breath, 'Father, you die a little more each day . . .'

And at last, out of his previously blocked, closed throat came the cry, but more than a cry it was the shrill wail of a wounded animal, followed, at once, by a rush of unstoppable, liberating tears.

*

A year before, when he'd been wounded in a shoot-out and ended up in the hospital, Livia had told him his father was phoning every day. He'd come only once to see him in person, when he was convalescing. He must have already been sick at the time. To Montalbano he'd merely looked a little thinner, nothing more. He was, in fact, even better dressed than usual, having always made a point of looking smart. On that occasion he'd asked his son if he needed anything. 'I can help,' he'd said.

*

When had they started to grow silently apart? His father had always been a caring, affectionate parent. That, Montalbano could not deny. He'd done everything in his power to lessen the pain of the loss of his mother. Whenever Montalbano fell ill as an adolescent — which luckily was not very often — his father used to stay at home from work so he wouldn't be alone. What was it, then, that hadn't worked? Perhaps there had always been a nearly total lack of communication between the two; they never could find the words to express their feelings for each other. So often, when very young, Montalbano had thought: *My father is a closed man.* And probably – though he realized it only now – his father had sat on a rock by the sea and thought the same of him. Still, he'd shown great sensitivity; before remarrying, for example, he'd waited for his son to finish university and win the placement competition. And yet when his father finally brought his new wife home, Montalbano had felt offended for no reason. A wall had risen between them; a glass wall, it's true, but a wall nonetheless. And so their meetings had gradually decreased in number to one or two a year. His father would usually arrive with a case of the wines produced by his vineyard, stay half a day, and then leave. Montalbano would always find the wine excellent and proudly offer it to his friends, telling them his father had made it. But had he ever told his father the wine was excellent? He dug deep in his memory. Never. Just as his father collected the newspapers that talked about him and felt like crying whenever he saw him on television, and yet had never, in person, congratulated him on the success of an investigation.

✴

He sat on that rock for over two hours, and when he got up to go back into town, his mind was made up. He would not go to visit his father. The sight of him would surely have made his father realize how gravely ill he was. It would have made things worse. Anyway, he didn't really know if his father would be happy to see him. Montalbano, moreover, had a fear, a horror, of the dying. He wasn't sure he could stand the fear and horror of seeing his father die. On the brink of collapse, he might run away.

*

When he got back to Marinella he still had that harsh, heavy feeling of weariness inside. He undressed, put on his bathing suit, and dived into the sea. He swam until his legs began to cramp. Returning home, he realized he was in no condition to go to the commissioner's for dinner.

'Hello? Montalbano here. I'm very sorry, but—'

'You can't come?'

'No, I'm really very sorry.'

'Work?'

Why not tell him the truth?

'No, Mr Commissioner. It's my father. Somebody sent me a letter. It looks like he's dying.'

At first the commissioner said nothing; the inspector only heard him heave a long sigh.

'Listen, Montalbano. If you want to go and see him, even for an extended stay, go ahead, don't worry about anything. I'll find a temporary replacement for you.'

'No, I'm not going. Thanks anyway.'

Again the commissioner didn't speak. He must have been shocked by the inspector's words; but he was a polite, old-fashioned man, and did not bring the subject up again.

'Montalbano, I feel awkward.'

'Please don't, not with me.'

'Do you remember I said I had two things to say to you at dinner?'

'Of course.'

'Well, I'll say them to you over the phone, even though, as I said, I feel awkward doing so. And this probably isn't the most appropriate moment, but I'm afraid you might find out from another source, like the newspapers . . . You don't know this, of course, but almost a year ago I put in a request for early retirement.'

'Oh God, don't tell me they—'

'Yes, they granted it.'

'But why do you want to retire?'

'Because I no longer feel in step with the world, and because I feel tired. To me, the betting service for soccer matches is still called Sisal.'

The inspector didn't understand.

'I'm sorry, I don't get it.'

'What do you call it?'

'Totocalcio.'

'You see? Therein lies the difference. A while ago, some journalist accused Montanelli of being too old, and as proof, he cited the fact that Montanelli still called Toto-calcio Sisal, as he used to call it thirty years ago.'

'But that doesn't mean anything! It was only a joke!'

'It means a lot, Montalbano, a lot. It means uncon-sciously holding on to the past, not wanting to see certain changes, even rejecting them. And I am barely a year away from retirement, anyway. I've still got my parents' house in La Spezia, which I've been having refurbished. If you like, when you come to Genoa to see Miss Livia, you can drop in on us.'

'And when are—'

'When am I leaving? What's today's date?'

'The twelfth of May.'

'I officially leave my job on the tenth of August.'

The commissioner cleared his throat, and the inspector understood that they had now come to the second thing, which was perhaps harder to say.

'About the other matter . . .'

He was hesitant, clearly. Montalbano bailed him out.

'It couldn't possibly be worse than what you just told me.'

'It's about your promotion.'

'No!'

'Listen to me, Montalbano. Your position can no longer be justified. In addition, now that I've been granted early retirement, I'm not, well, in a strong bargaining position. I have to recommend your promotion, and there won't be any obstacles.'

'Will I be transferred?'

'There's a ninety-nine percent chance of it. Bear in mind that if I didn't recommend you for the appointment, with all your successes, the ministry might see that in a negative light and could end up transferring you anyway, but without a promotion. Couldn't you use a raise?'

The inspector's brain was running at full speed, smoking, in fact, trying to find a possible solution. He glimpsed one and pounced on it.

'And what if, from this moment on, I no longer arrested anyone?'

'I don't understand.'

'I mean, what if I pretend not to solve any more cases, if I mishandle investigations, if I let slip—'

'Rubbish, Montalbano, the only thing you're letting slip is idiocies. I just don't understand. Every time I talk to you about promotion, you suddenly regress and start reasoning like a child.'

※

He killed an hour lolling about the house, putting some books back on the shelf and dusting the glass over the five engravings he owned, which Adelina never did. He did not turn on the television. He looked at his watch: almost ten p.m. He got in his car and drove to Montelusa. The three cinemas were showing the Taviani brothers' *Elective Affinities*, Bertolucci's *Stealing Beauty*, and *Travels with Goofy*. Without the slightest hesitation, he chose the cartoon. The cinema was empty. He went back to the man who had torn his ticket.

'There's nobody there!'

'You're there. What do you want, company? It's late. At this hour, all the little kids are asleep. You're the only one still awake.'

He had so much fun that, at one moment, he caught himself laughing out loud in the empty cinema.

✻

There comes a moment, he thought, *when you realize your life has changed. But when did it happen? you ask yourself. And you have no answer. Unnoticed events kept accumulating until, one day, a transformation occurred — or perhaps they were perfectly visible events, whose importance and consequences, however, you never took into account. You ask yourself over and over, but the answer to that 'when' never comes. As if it mattered!*

Montalbano, for his part, had a precise answer to that question. My life changed, he would have said, on the twelfth of May.

✻

Beside the front door to his house, Montalbano had recently had a small lamp installed that went on automatically when night fell. It was by the light of this lamp that he saw, from the main road, a car stopped in the clearing in front of the house. He turned into the small lane leading to the house, and pulled up a few inches from the other car. As he expected, it was a metallic grey BMW. Its number plate was AM 237 GW. But there wasn't a soul to be seen. The man who'd driven it there was surely hiding somewhere nearby. Montalbano decided it was best to feign indifference. He stepped out of the car, whistling, closed the door, and saw somebody waiting for him. He hadn't noticed him earlier because the man was standing on the far side of the car and was so small in stature that his head did not exceed the height of the car's roof. Practically a midget, or not much more than one. Well dressed, and wearing small, gold-rimmed glasses.

'You've made me wait a long time,' the little man said, coming forward.

Montalbano, keys in hand, moved towards the front door. The quasi-midget stepped in front of him, shaking a kind of identity card.

'My papers,' he said.

The inspector pushed aside the little hand holding the documents, opened the door, and went inside. The man followed behind him.

'I am Colonel Lohengrin Pera,' said the elf.

The inspector stopped dead in his tracks, as if someone had pressed the barrel of a gun between his shoulder blades. He turned slowly around and looked the colonel up and down. His parents must have given him that name to compensate somehow for his stature and surname. Montalbano felt fascinated by the colonel's little shoes, which he must surely have had made to measure; they wouldn't even have fitted in the 'sottouomo' category, as the shoemakers called it – that is, for 'sub-men'. And yet the services had enlisted him, so he must have been tall enough to make the grade. His eyes, however, behind the lenses, were lively, attentive, dangerous. Montalbano felt certain he was looking at the brains behind the Moussa affair. He went into the kitchen, still followed by the colonel, put the mullets in tomato sauce that Adelina had made for him into the oven, and started setting the table, without once opening his mouth. On the table was a seven-hundred-page book he'd bought from a bookshop and had never opened. He'd been drawn by the title: *The Metaphysics of Partial Being*. He picked it up, stood on tiptoe, and put it on the shelf, pressing the button on the videocamera. As if somebody had said 'roll 'em'. Colonel Lohengrin Pera sat down in the right chair.

EIGHTEEN

Montalbano took a good half hour to eat his mullets, either because he wanted to savour them as they deserved, or to give the colonel the impression that he didn't give a flying fuck about what the man might have to say to him. He didn't even offer him a glass of wine. He acted as if he were alone, to the point where he even once burped out loud. For his part, Lohengrin Pera, once he'd sat down, had stopped moving, limiting himself to staring at the inspector with beady, snake-like eyes. Only when Montalbano had downed a demi-tasse of espresso did the colonel begin to speak.

'You understand, of course, why I've come to see you.'

The inspector stood up, went into the kitchen, placed the little cup in the sink, and returned.

'I'm playing above board,' the colonel continued, after waiting for him to return. 'It's probably the best way, with you. That's why I chose to come in that car, for which you twice requested information on the owner.'

From his jacket pocket he withdrew two sheets of paper,

which Montalbano recognized as the faxes he'd sent to
Vehicle Registration.

'Only you already knew who the car belonged to; your
commissioner must certainly have told you its number plate
was cloaked. So, since you sent me these faxes anyway, it
must mean their intention was more than simply to request
information, however imprudently. I therefore became
convinced – correct me if I'm wrong – that for your own
reasons, you wanted us to come out into the open. So here
I am: your wish has been granted.'

'Would you excuse me a minute?' Montalbano asked.

Without waiting for an answer, he got up, went into
the kitchen and returned with a plate on which was a huge,
hard piece of Sicilian *cassata* ice cream. The colonel settled
in patiently and waited for him to eat it.

'Please continue,' said the inspector. 'I can't eat it when
it's like this. It has to melt a little first.'

'Before we go any further,' resumed the colonel, who
apparently had very strong nerves, 'let me clarify something.
In your second fax, you mention the murder of a woman
named Aisha. We had absolutely nothing to do with that
death. It must surely have been an unfortunate accident.
If she'd needed to be eliminated, we would have done so
immediately.'

'I don't doubt it. I was well aware of that too.'

'So why did you state otherwise in your fax?'

'Just to turn up the heat.'

'Right. Have you read the writings and speeches of
Mussolini?'

'He's not one of my favourite authors.'

'In one of his last writings, Mussolini says that the people should be treated like a donkey, with a carrot and a stick.'

'Always so original, that Mussolini! You know something?'

'What?'

'My grandfather used to say the same thing. He was a peasant and, since he wasn't Mussolini, he was referring only to the ass, the donkey, that is.'

'May I continue the metaphor?'

'By all means!'

'Your faxes, as well as your having persuaded Vice-Commissioner Valente of Mazàra to interrogate the captain of the fishing boat and the head of the prefect's cabinet, these and other things were the stick you used to flush us out.'

'So where does the carrot come in?'

'The carrot is in the declarations you made at the press conference you held after arresting Mrs Lapècora for the murder of her husband. You could have dragged us into that one by the hair, but you didn't. You were careful to keep that crime within the confines of jealousy and greed. Still, that was a menacing carrot; it said—'

'Colonel, I suggest you drop the metaphor; at this point we've got a talking carrot.'

'Fine. You, with that press conference, wanted us to know that you had other information in your possession which, at that moment, you were unwilling to show. Am I right?'

The inspector extended a spoon towards the ice cream, filled it, and brought it to his mouth.

'It's still hard,' he said to Lohengrin Pera.

'You discourage me,' the colonel commented, but he went on. 'Anyway, since we're laying our cards on the table, will you tell me everything you know about the case?'

'What case?'

'The killing of Ahmed Moussa.'

He'd succeeded in making him say that name openly, as duly recorded by the tape in the video camera.

'No.'

'Why not?'

'Because I love the sound of your voice, the way you speak.'

'May I have a glass of water?'

To all appearances, Lohengrin Pera was perfectly calm and controlled, but inside he was surely close to the boiling point. The request for water was a clear sign.

'Go and get it yourself from the kitchen.'

While the colonel fussed about in the kitchen with the glass and tap, Montalbano, who was looking at him from behind, noticed a bulge under his jacket, beside the right buttock. Want to bet the midget is armed with a gun twice his size? He decided not to take any chances and brought a very sharp knife, which he had used to cut the bread, closer to him.

'I'll be explicit and brief,' Lohengrin Pera began, sitting

down and wiping his lips with a tiny handkerchief, an embroidered postage stamp. 'A little more than two years ago, our counterparts in Tunis asked us to collaborate with them on a delicate operation aimed at neutralizing a dangerous terrorist, whose name you got me to say just a moment ago.'

'I'm sorry,' said Montalbano, 'but I have a very limited vocabulary. By "neutralizing" do you mean "physically eliminating"?'

'Call it whatever you like. We discussed the matter with our superiors, naturally, and were ordered not to collaborate. But then, less than a month later, we found ourselves in a very unpleasant position, where it was we who had to ask our friends in Tunis for help.'

'What a coincidence!' Montalbano exclaimed.

'Yes. Without any questions, they gave us the help we wanted, and so we found ourselves morally indebted—'

'No!' Montalbano yelled.

Lohengrin Pera gave a start.

'What's wrong?' he asked.

'You said: *morally* indebted.'

'As you wish. Let's say merely "indebted", without the adverb, all right? But excuse me; before going on, I have to make a telephone call. I keep forgetting.'

'Be my guest,' the inspector said, gesturing towards the phone.

'Thanks; I've got a mobile phone.'

Lohengrin Pera was not armed. The bulge on his

buttock was his mobile phone. He punched in a number that Montalbano was unable to read.

'Hello? This is Pera. All's well, we're talking.'

He turned off the phone and left it on the table.

'Our colleagues in Tunis discovered that Ahmed's favourite sister, Karima, had been living in Sicily for years, and that, through her work, she had a vast circle of acquaintances.'

'Vast, no,' Montalbano corrected him. 'Select, yes. She was a respectable prostitute; she inspired confidence.'

'Ahmed's right-hand man, Fahrid, suggested to his chief that they establish a base of operations in Sicily and avail themselves of Karima's services. Ahmed rather trusted Fahrid; he didn't know he'd been bought by the Tunisian secret services. With our discreet assistance, Fahrid came here and made contact with Karima, who, after a careful review of her clients, chose Lapècora. Perhaps by threatening to inform his wife of their relationship, Karima forced Lapècora to reopen his old import-export business, which turned out to be an excellent cover. Fahrid was able to communicate with Ahmed by writing coded business letters to an imaginary company in Tunis. By the way, in your press conference you said that at a certain point Lapècora wrote anonymously to his wife, informing her of his liaison. Why did he do that?'

'Because he smelled something fishy in the whole arrangement.'

'Do you think he suspected the truth?'

'Of course not! At the most, he probably thought they

were trafficking drugs. If he'd discovered he was at the centre of an international intrigue, he'd have been killed on the spot.'

'I agree. At first, our primary concern was to keep the impatience of the Tunisians in check. But we also wanted to be certain that, once we put the bait in the water, the fish would bite.'

'Excuse me, but who was the blond young man who showed up now and then with Fahrid?'

The colonel looked at him with admiration.

'You know that too? He's one of our men who would periodically go and check up on things.'

'And while he was at it, he would fuck Karima.'

'These things happen. Finally, Fahrid persuaded Ahmed to come to Italy by tempting him with the prospect of a big weapons shipment. As always with our invisible protection, Ahmed Moussa arrived at Mazàra, according to Fahrid's instructions. Under pressure from the chief of the prefect's cabinet, the captain of the fishing boat agreed to take Ahmed aboard, since the meeting between Ahmed and the imaginary arms dealer was supposed to take place on the open sea. Without the slightest suspicion, Ahmed Moussa walked into the trap. He even lit a cigarette, as he'd been told to do, so that they might better recognize each other. But Commendatore Spadaccia, the cabinet chief, made a big mistake.'

'He hadn't warned the captain that it would not be a clandestine meeting, but an ambush,' said Montalbano.

'You could say that. The captain, as he'd been told to

do, threw Ahmed's papers into the sea and divided the seventy million lire the Arab had in his pocket with the rest of the crew. Then, instead of returning to Mazàra, he changed course. He had his doubts about us.'

'Oh?'

'You see, we had steered our motor patrols away from the scene of the action, and the captain knew this. If that's the situation, he must have thought, who's to say I won't run into something on the way back in – a missile, a mine, even another motor patrol that would sink my boat to destroy all trace of the operation? That's why he came to Vigàta. He was shuffling the cards.'

'Had he guessed right?'

'In what sense?'

'Was there someone or something waiting for the fishing boat?'

'Come now, Montalbano! That would have been a useless massacre!'

'And you engage only in useful massacres, is that it? And how do you plan to keep the crew quiet?'

'With the carrot and the stick, to quote again that writer you don't appreciate. In any case, I've said everything I had to say.'

'No.'

'What do you mean, no?'

'I mean: that's not everything. You have very cleverly taken me out to sea, but I haven't forgotten those left behind on land. Fahrid, for example. He must have learned, from one of your informers, that Ahmed had been killed;

but the fishing boat had docked at Vigàta, inexplicably — for him. This troubled him. At any rate, he must now proceed to the second part of his assignment. That is, neutralizing, as you put it, Lapècora. So he shows up at the man's front door and, to his amazement and alarm, finds out that somebody got there first. And so he shits in his pants.'

'I beg your pardon?'

'He gets scared, he no longer knows what is happening. Like the captain of the fishing boat, he thinks your people are behind it. It looks to him like you've begun removing from circulation everyone who was in some way involved in the operation. For a moment, perhaps, he suspects it might have been Karima who did away with Lapècora. You may not know this, but Karima, under orders from Fahrid, forced Lapècora to hide her in his apartment; Fahrid didn't want Lapècora to get any brilliant ideas during those critical hours. Fahrid, however, didn't know that once she'd carried out her mission, Karima had gone back home. In any event, at some point that morning, Fahrid met up with Karima, and the two must have had a violent argument in the course of which he told her that her brother had been killed. Karima then tried to escape. She failed, and she was murdered. She would have had to be eliminated anyway, at some later point, on the quiet.'

'As I'd suspected,' said Lohengrin Pera, 'you've worked it all out. Now I ask you to pause and think. You, like me, are a loyal, devoted servant of our state. And so—'

'Stick it up your arse,' Montalbano said softly.

'I don't understand.'

'Let me repeat: you can take our state and stick it up your arse. You and I have diametrically opposed concepts of what it means to be a servant of the state. For all intents and purposes, we serve two different states. So I beg you please not to liken your work to mine.'

'So now you want to play Don Quixote, Montalbano? Every community needs someone to clean the toilets. But this does not mean that those who clean the toilets are not part of the community.'

Montalbano felt his rage growing; one more word would surely have been a mistake. He reached out with one hand, brought the dish of ice cream nearer, and began to eat. By now Lohengrin Pera had got used to the ritual, and once Montalbano started nibbling the ice cream, he stopped talking.

'Karima was killed, correct?' asked Montalbano after a few spoonfuls.

'Unfortunately, yes. Fahrid was afraid that—'

'I'm not interested in why. I'm interested in the fact that she was killed by the authority of a loyal servant of the state such as yourself. What would you call this specific case: neutralization or murder?'

'Montalbano, you can't use the standard of common morality—'

'Colonel, I already warned you once: do not speak of morality in my presence.'

'I merely meant that sometimes, the reason of state—'

'That's enough,' said Montalbano, who had wolfed

down the ice cream in four angry bites. Then, suddenly, he slapped his forehead.

'What time is it, anyway?'

The colonel looked at his wristwatch, a dainty, precious item that looked like a child's toy.

'It's already two o'clock.'

'Why on earth hasn't Fazio arrived?' Montalbano asked himself, pretending to be worried. Then he added, 'I have to make a phone call.'

He got up, went over to the phone on his desk two yards away, and started speaking in a loud voice so that Lohengrin Pera would hear everything.

'Hello, Fazio? Montalbano here.'

Fazio, drowsy with sleep, spoke with difficulty.

'Chief. What is it?'

'Come on, did you forget about the arrest?'

'What arrest?' said Fazio, at sea.

'The arrest of Simone Fileccia.'

Simone Fileccia had been arrested the day before, by Fazio himself. And, in fact, Fazio understood at once.

'What should I do?'

'Come and pick me up at my place, and we'll go and get him.'

'Should I bring my own car?'

'No, better make it a squad car.'

'I'll be right there.'

'Wait.'

The inspector put his hand over the receiver and turned to the colonel.

'How much more time will this take?'

'That's up to you,' said Lohengrin Pera.

'Be here in, say, twenty minutes or so,' the inspector said to Fazio, 'not before. I have to finish talking to a friend.'

He hung up, sat back down. The colonel smiled.

'Since we've got so little time, tell me your price immediately, if you'll forgive the expression.'

'I come cheap, very cheap,' said Montalbano.

'I'm listening.'

'Two things, that's all. Within a week, I want Karima's body to turn up, and in such a way that there can be no mistake as to its identification.'

A billy club to the head would have had less effect on Lohengrin Pera. Opening and closing his mouth, he gripped the edge of the table with his tiny hands, as if afraid he might fall out of his chair.

'Why?' he managed to utter with the voice of a silk-worm.

'None of your fucking business,' was the firm, blunt reply.

The colonel shook his little head from left to right and right to left, looking like a spring puppet.

'It's not possible.'

'Why?'

'We don't know where she was . . . buried.'

'And who does know?'

'Fahrid.'

'Has Fahrid been neutralized? You know, I'm starting to like that word.'

'No. He's gone back to Tunisia.'

'Then there's no problem. Just get in touch with his playmates in Tunis.'

'No,' the midget said firmly. 'The matter has been put to rest at this point. We have nothing to gain by stirring things up again with the discovery of a corpse. No, it's not possible. Ask me anything you like, but that is one thing we cannot grant you. Aside from the fact that I can't see the purpose of it.'

'Too bad,' said Montalbano, getting up. Automatically, Lohengrin Pera also stood up, in spite of himself. But he wasn't the type to give in easily.

'Well, just for curiosity's sake, would you tell me what your second demand is?'

'Certainly. The commissioner of Vigàta has put in a request for my promotion to vice-commissioner—'

'We shall have no problem whatsoever having it accepted,' said the colonel, relieved.

'What about having it rejected?'

Montalbano could distinctly hear Lohengrin Pera's world crumble and fall to pieces on top of him, and he saw the colonel hunch over as if trying to shield himself from a sudden explosion.

'You are totally insane,' said the colonel, sincerely terrified.

'You've just noticed?'

'Listen, you can do whatever you like, but I cannot give in to your demand to turn up the body. Absolutely not.'

'Shall we see how the tape came out?' Montalbano asked politely.

'What tape?' said Lohengrin Pera, confused.

Montalbano went over to the bookcase, stood up on tiptoe, took out the video camera, and showed it to the colonel.

'Jesus!' said the colonel, collapsing in a chair. He was sweating. 'Montalbano, for your own good, I implore you . . .'

But the man was a snake, and he behaved like a snake. As he appeared to be begging the inspector not to do anything stupid, his hand had moved ever so slightly and was now within reach of the mobile phone. Fully aware that he would never make it out of there alone, he wanted to call for reinforcements. Montalbano let him get another centimetre closer to the phone, then sprang. With one hand he sent the phone flying from the table, with the other he struck the colonel hard in the face. Lohengrin Pera flew all the way across the room, glasses falling, then slammed against the far wall back first, and slid to the ground. Montalbano slowly drew near and, as he'd seen done in a movie about Nazis, crushed the colonel's little glasses with his heel.

NINETEEN

And while he was at it, he went for broke, pounding the mobile phone violently into the ground with his heel until he'd half-pulverized it.

He finished the job with a hammer he kept in his tool drawer. Then he approached the colonel, who was still on the floor, groaning feebly. As soon as he saw the inspector in front of him, Lohengrin Pera shielded his face with his forearms, as children do.

'Enough, for pity's sake,' he implored.

What kind of man was he? A punch in the face and a trickle of blood from his split lip, and he's reduced to this? Montalbano grabbed him by the lapels of his jacket, lifted him up, and sat him down. With a trembling hand, Lohengrin Pera wiped away the blood with his embroidered postage stamp, closed his eyes, and appeared to faint.

'It's just that . . . blood . . . I can't stand the sight of it,' he muttered.

'Yours or other people's?' Montalbano enquired.

He went into the kitchen, grabbed a half-full bottle of whisky and a glass, and set these in front of the colonel.

'I'm a teetotaller.'

Montalbano felt a little calmer now, having let off some steam.

If the colonel, he thought, wanted to phone for help, then the people who were supposed to come to his rescue must certainly be in the neighbourhood, just a few minutes' drive from the house. That was the real danger. He heard the doorbell ring.

'Chief? It's me, Fazio.'

He opened the door halfway.

'Listen, Fazio, I have to finish talking to that person I mentioned. Wait in the car. I'll call you when I need you. But be careful: there may be some people in the area who are up to no good. Stop anyone you see approaching the house.'

He shut the door and sat back down in front of Lohengrin Pera, who seemed lost in dejection.

'Now try to understand me, because soon you won't be able to understand anything anymore.'

'What do you intend to do to me?' asked the colonel, turning pale.

'No blood, don't worry. I've got you in the palm of my hand, I hope you realize that. You were foolish enough to blab the whole story in front of a video camera. If I have the tape aired on TV, it's going to kick up such a fucking row on the international scene that you'll be selling chickpea sandwiches on a street corner before it's all over. If, on the other hand, you let Karima's body be found and block my promotion — and make no mistake, the two things go hand in hand — I give you my word of honour that I'll destroy the tape. You have no choice but to trust me. Have I made myself clear?'

Lohengrin Pera nodded his little head 'yes', and at that moment the inspector realized that the knife had disappeared from the table. The colonel must have seized it when he was talking to Fazio.

'Tell me something,' said Montalbano. 'Are there such things, that you know of, as poisonous worms?'

Pera gave him a questioning look.

'For your own good, put down the knife you're holding inside your jacket.'

Without a word, the colonel obeyed and set the knife down on the table. Montalbano opened the whisky bottle, filled the glass to the brim, and held it out to Lohengrin Pera, who recoiled with a grimace of disgust.

'I've already told you I'm a teetotaller.'

'Drink.'

'I can't, believe me.'

Squeezing the colonel's cheeks with the thumb and forefinger of his left hand, Montalbano forced him to open his mouth.

*

Fazio heard the inspector call for him after waiting some forty-five minutes in the car, as he was starting to drift off into a leaden sleep. Upon entering the house, he immediately saw a drunken midget, who had vomited all over himself to boot. Unable to stand on his feet, the midget, leaning first against a chair and then against the wall, was trying to sing 'Celeste Aida'. On the floor, Fazio noticed a pair of glasses and a mobile phone, both smashed to pieces. On the table were an empty bottle of whisky, a glass, also empty, and three or four sheets of paper and some identity cards.

'Listen closely, Fazio,' said the inspector. 'I'm going to tell you exactly what happened here, in case anybody questions you. I was returning home this evening, around midnight, when I saw, at the top of the lane that leads to my house, this man's car, a BMW, blocking my path. He was completely drunk. I brought him home with me because he was in no condition to drive. He had no identification in his pockets, nothing. After several attempts to sober him up, I called you for help.'

'Got it,' said Fazio.

'Now, here's the plan. You're going to pick him up – he doesn't weigh much, in any case – put him in his BMW, get behind the wheel, and put him in a holding cell. I'll follow behind you in the squad car.'

'And how are you going to get back home afterwards?'

'You'll have to drive me back. Sorry. Tomorrow morning, as soon as you see he's recovered his senses, you're to set him free.'

✳

ANDREA CAMILLERI

Back at home, he removed the pistol from the glove compartment of his car where he always kept it, and stuck it in his belt. Then he took a broom and swept up all the fragments of Lohengrin Pera's mobile phone and glasses, and wrapped them in a sheet of newspaper. He took the little shovel that Mimì had given François and dug two deep holes almost directly below the veranda. In one he put the bundle and covered it up, in the other he dumped the papers and documents, now shredded into little pieces. These he sprinkled with petrol and set on fire. When they had turned to ash, he covered up this hole as well. The sky was beginning to lighten. He went into the kitchen, brewed a pot of strong coffee and drank it. Then he shaved and took a shower. He wanted to be completely relaxed when he sat down to enjoy the video tape.

He put the little cassette inside the bigger one, as Nicolò had instructed him to do, then turned on the TV and the VCR. After a few seconds with the screen still blank, he got up and checked the appliances, certain he'd made some wrong connection. He was utterly hopeless with this sort of thing, to say nothing of computers, which terrified him. Nothing doing this time, either. He popped out the larger cassette, opened it, looked at it. The little cassette seemed poorly inserted, so he pushed it all the way in. He put the whole package back into the VCR. Still nothing on the damn screen. What the hell wasn't working? As he was asking himself this, he froze, seized by doubt. He dashed to the phone.

'Hello?' answered the voice at the other end, pro-
nouncing each letter with tremendous effort.

'Nicolò? This is Montalbano.'

'Who the hell else could it be, Jesus fucking Christ?'

'I have to ask you something.'

'Do you know what time it is?'

'I'm sorry, really sorry. Remember the video camera you
lent me?'

'Yeah?'

'Which button was I supposed to push to record? The
top one or the bottom one?'

'The top one, arsehole.'

He'd pushed the wrong button.

✻

He got undressed again, put on his bathing suit, bravely
entered the freezing water, and began to swim. After tiring
and turning over to float on his back, he started thinking
that it was not, in the end, so terrible that he hadn't
recorded anything. The important thing was that the
colonel believed he had and would continue to do so. He
returned to shore, went back in the house, threw himself
down on the bed, still wet, and fell asleep.

✻

When he woke up it was past nine, and he had the distinct
impression he couldn't go back to work and resume his
everyday chores. He decided to inform Mimì.

'Hallo! Hallo! Whoozat talkin' onna line?'

'It's Montalbano, Cat.'

'Izzat really 'n' truly you in person, sir?'

'It's really and truly me in person. Let me speak with Inspector Augello.'

'Hello, Salvo. Where are you?'

'At home. Listen, Mimì, I don't think I can come in to work.'

'Are you sick?'

'No. I just don't feel up to it, not today nor tomorrow. I need to rest for four or five days. Can you cover for me?'

'Of course.'

'Thanks.'

'Wait. Don't hang up.'

'What is it?'

'I'm a little concerned, Salvo. You've been acting weird for the last couple of days. What's the matter with you? Don't make me start worrying about you.'

'Mimì, I just need a little rest, that's all.'

'Where will you go?'

'I don't know yet. I'll phone you later.'

*

Actually, he knew exactly where he would go. He packed his bag in five minutes, then took a little longer to select which books to take along. He left a note in block letters for Adelina, the housekeeper, informing her he'd be back within a week. When he arrived at the trattoria in Mazàra, they greeted him like the prodigal son.

'The other day, I believe I understood that you rent rooms.'

'Yes, we've got five upstairs. But it's the off-season now, so only one of 'em's rented.'

They showed him a room, spacious and bright and looking straight onto the sea.

He lay down on the bed, brain emptied of thoughts, chest swelling with a kind of happy melancholy. He was loosing the moorings, ready to sail out to the country of sleep, when he heard a knock on the door.

'Come in, it's unlocked.'

The cook appeared in the doorway. He was a big man of considerable heft, about forty, with dark eyes and skin.

'What are you doing? Aren't you coming down? I heard you were here and so I made something for you that . . .'

What the cook had made, Montalbano couldn't hear, because a sweet, soft melody, a heavenly tune, had started playing in his ears.

＊

For the last hour he'd been watching a rowing boat slowly approaching the shore. On it was a man rowing in sharply rhythmic, vigorous strokes. The boat had also been sighted by the owner of the trattoria; Montalbano heard him cry out, 'Luicì! The cavaliere's coming back!'

The inspector then saw Luicino, the restaurateur's sixteen-year-old son, enter the water to push the boat up onto the sand so the passenger wouldn't get his feet wet. The cavaliere, whose name Montalbano did not know, was smartly dressed, tie and all. On his head he wore a white Panama hat, with the requisite black band.

'Cavaliere, did you catch anything?' the restaurateur asked him.

'A pain in the arse, that's what I caught.'

He was a thin, nervy man, about seventy years old. Later, Montalbano heard him bustling about in the room next to his.

*

'I set a table over here,' said the cook as soon as Montalbano appeared for dinner, and he led him into a tiny room with space for only two tables. The inspector felt grateful for this, since the big dining room was booming with the voices and laughter of a large gathering.

'I've set it for two,' the cook continued. 'Do you have any objection if Cavaliere Pintacuda eats with you?'

He certainly did have an objection: he feared he would have to talk while eating.

A few minutes later, the gaunt septuagenarian introduced himself with a bow.

'Liborio Pintacuda, and I'm not a cavaliere,' he said, sitting down. 'There's something I must tell you, even at the risk of appearing rude,' the non-cavaliere continued. 'I, when I'm talking, do not eat. Conversely, when I'm eating, I don't talk.'

'Welcome to the club,' said Montalbano, sighing with relief.

The pasta with crab was as graceful as a first-rate

ballerina, but the stuffed bass in saffron sauce left him breathless, almost frightened.

'Do you think this kind of miracle could ever happen again?' he asked Pintacuda, gesturing towards his now empty plate. They had both finished and therefore recovered the power of speech.

'It'll happen again, don't worry, just like the miracle of the blood of San Gennaro,' said Pintacuda. 'I've been coming here for years, and never, I repeat, never, has Tanino's cooking let me down.'

'At a top-notch restaurant, a chef like Tanino would be worth his weight in gold,' the inspector commented.

'Yes he would. Last year, a Frenchman passed this way, the owner of a famous Parisian restaurant. He practically got down on his knees and begged Tanino to come to Paris with him. But there was no persuading him. Tanino says this is where he's from, and this is where he'll die.'

'Someone must surely have taught him to cook like that. He can't have been born with that gift.'

'You know, up until ten years ago, Tanino was a small-time crook. Petty theft, drug dealing. Always in and out of jail. Then, one night, the Blessed Virgin appeared to him.'

'Are you joking?'

'I try hard not to. As he tells it, the Virgin took his hands in hers, looked him in the eye, and declared that from the next day forward, he would become a great chef.'

'Come on!'

'You, for example, knew nothing of this story of the Virgin, and yet after eating the bass, you specifically used the word "miracle". But I can see you don't believe in the supernatural, so I'll change subject. What brings you to these parts, Inspector?'

Montalbano gave a start. He hadn't told anyone there what he did for a living.

'I saw your press conference on television, after you arrested that woman for killing her husband,' Pintacuda explained.

'Please don't tell anybody who I am.'

'But they all know who you are, Inspector. Since they've gathered that you don't like to be recognized, however, they play dumb.'

'And what do you do of interest?'

'I used to be a professor of philosophy. If you can call teaching philosophy interesting.'

'Isn't it?'

'Not at all. The students get bored. They no longer care enough to learn how Hegel or Kant thought about things. Philosophy should probably be replaced with some subject like, I don't know, "Basic Management". Then it still might mean something.'

'Basic management of what?'

'Life, my friend. Do you know what Benedetto Croce writes in his *Memoirs*? He says that he learned from experience to consider life a serious matter, as a problem to be solved. Seems obvious, doesn't it? But it's not. One would have to explain to young people, philosophically, what it means, for example, to smash their car into another car one Saturday night. And to tell them how, philosophically, this

could be avoided. But we'll have time to discuss all this. I'm
told you'll be staying here a few days.'

'Yes. Do you live alone?'

'For the fifteen days I spend here, very much alone.
The rest of the time I live in a big old house in Trapani
with my wife and four daughters, all married, and eight
grandchildren, who, when they're not at school, are with
me all day. At least once every three months I escape and
come here, leaving no phone number or forwarding address.
I cleanse myself, take the waters of solitude. For me this
place is like a clinic where I detoxify myself of an excess
of sentiment. Do you play chess?'

*

On the afternoon of the following day, as he was lying in
bed reading Sciascia's *Council of Egypt* for the twentieth time,
it occurred to him that he'd forgotten to tell Valente about
the odd agreement he'd made with the colonel. The matter
might prove dangerous for his colleague in Mazàra if he
were to continue investigating. He went downstairs where
there was a telephone.

'Valente? Montalbano here.'

'Salvo, where the hell are you? I asked for you at the
office and they said they had no news of you.'

'Why were you looking for me? Has something come
up?'

'Yes. The commissioner called me out of the blue this
morning to tell me my request for a transfer had been
accepted. They're sending me to Sestri.'

Valente's wife, Giulia, was from Sestri, and her parents also lived there. Until now, every time the vice-commissioner had asked to be transferred to Liguria, his request had been denied.

'Didn't I say that something good would come out of this affair?' Montalbano reminded him.

'Do you think——?'

'Of course. They're getting you out of their hair, in such a way that you won't object. And they're right. When does the transfer take effect?'

'Immediately.'

'See? I'll come and say goodbye before you leave.'

Lohengrin Pera and his little gang of playmates had moved very fast. It remained to be seen whether this was a good or a bad sign. He needed to do a foolproof test. If they were in such a hurry to put the matter to rest, then surely they had wasted no time in sending him a message as well. The Italian bureaucracy, usually slow as a snail, becomes lightning-quick when it comes to screwing the citizen. With this well-known truth in mind, he called his commissioner.

'Montalbano! For God's sake, where have you run off to?'

'Sorry for not letting you know. I've taken a few days off to rest.'

'I understand. You went to see——'

'No. Were you looking for me? Do you need me?'

'Yes, I was looking for you, but I don't need you for

anything. Just rest. Do you remember I was supposed to recommend you for a promotion?'

'How could I forget?'

'Well, this morning Commendator Ragusa called me from the Ministry of Justice. He's a good friend of mine. He told me that, apparently . . . some obstacles have come up — of what kind, I have no idea. In short, your promotion has been blocked. Ragusa wouldn't, or couldn't, tell me any more than that. He also made it clear that it was useless, and perhaps even unwise, to insist. Believe me, I'm shocked and offended.'

'Not me.'

'Don't I know it! In fact, you're happy, aren't you?'

'Doubly happy, Commissioner.'

'Doubly?'

'I'll explain when I see you in person.'

He set his mind at rest. They were moving in the right direction.

※

The following morning, Liborio Pintacuda, a steaming cup of coffee in hand, woke the inspector up when it was still dark outside.

'I'll wait for you in the boat.'

He'd invited him to a useless half day of fishing, and the inspector had accepted. Montalbano put on a pair of jeans and a long-sleeved shirt. Sitting in a boat with a gentleman dressed to the nines, he would have felt silly in a bathing suit.

Fishing, for the professor, proved to be exactly like eating. He never opened his mouth, except, every now and then, to curse the fish for not biting.

Around nine in the morning, with the sun already high in the sky, Montalbano couldn't hold back any longer.

'I'm losing my father,' he said.

'My condolences,' the professor said without looking up from his fishing line.

The words seemed flat and inappropriate to the inspector.

'He hasn't died yet. He's dying,' he clarified.

'It makes no difference. For you, your father died the very moment you learned he was going to die. Everything else is, so to speak, a bodily formality. Nothing more. Does he live with you?'

'No, he's in another town.'

'By himself?'

'Yes. And I can't summon the courage to go and see him in this state, before he goes. I just can't. The very idea scares me. I'll never have the strength to set foot in the hospital where he's staying.'

The old man said nothing, limiting himself to replacing the bait the fish had eaten with many thanks. Then he decided to talk.

'You know, I happen to have followed an investigation of yours, the one about the "terracotta dog". In that instance, you abandoned an investigation into some weapons trafficking to throw yourself heart and soul into tracking a crime from fifty years ago, even though solving it wasn't going to yield any practical results. Do you know why you did it?'

'Out of curiosity?' Montalbano guessed.

'No, my friend. It was a very shrewd, intelligent way for you to keep practising your unpleasant profession, but by escaping from everyday reality. Apparently this everyday reality sometimes becomes too much for you to bear. And so you escape. As I do when I take refuge here. But the moment I go back home, I immediately lose half of the benefit. The fact of your father's dying is real, but you refuse to confirm it by seeing it in person. You're like the child who thinks he can blot out the world by closing his eyes.'

Professor Liborio Pintacuda, at this point, looked the inspector straight in the eye.

'When will you decide to grow up?'

TWENTY

As he was going downstairs for supper, he decided he would head back to Vigàta the following morning. He'd been away for five days. Luicino had set the table in the usual little room, and Pintacuda was already sitting at his place and waiting for him.

'I'm leaving tomorrow,' Montalbano announced.

'Not me. I need another week of detox.'

Luicino brought the first course at once, and thereafter their mouths were used only for eating. When the second course arrived, they had a surprise.

'Meatballs!' the professor exclaimed, indignant. 'Meatballs are for dogs!'

The inspector kept his cool. The aroma floating up from the dish and into his nose was rich and dense.

'What's with Tanino? Is he sick?' Pintacuda enquired with a tone of concern.

'No sir, he's in the kitchen,' replied Luicino.

Only then did the professor break a meatball in half with his fork and bring it to his mouth. Montalbano hadn't yet made a move. Pintacuda chewed slowly, eyes half closed, and emitted a sort of moan.

'If one ate something like this at death's door, he'd be happy even to go to hell,' he said softly.

The inspector put half a meatball in his mouth, and with his tongue and palate began a scientific analysis that would have put Jacomuzzi to shame. So: fish and, no question, onion, hot pepper, whisked eggs, salt, pepper, breadcrumbs. But two other flavours, hiding under the taste of the butter used in the frying, hadn't yet answered the call. At the second mouthful, he recognized what had escaped him in the first: cumin and coriander.

'*Koftas!*' he shouted in amazement.

'What did you say?' asked Pintacuda.

'We're eating an Indian dish, executed to perfection.'

'I don't give a damn where it's from,' said the professor. 'I only know it's a dream. And please don't speak to me again until I've finished eating.'

*

Pintacuda waited for the table to be cleared and then suggested they play their now customary game of chess that, equally customarily, Montalbano always lost.

'Excuse me a minute; first I'd like to say goodbye to Tanino.'

'I'll come with you.'

The cook was in the process of giving his assistant a serious tongue-lashing for having cleaned the pans poorly.

'When you do that, they end up tasting like yesterday's food and nobody can tell what they're eating anymore.'

'Listen,' said Montalbano, 'is it true you've never been outside Sicily?'

He must have inadvertently assumed a policeman-like tone, because Tanino seemed suddenly to have returned to his days as a delinquent.

'Never, Inspector, I swear! I got witnesses!'

Therefore he could never have learned that dish from some foreign restaurant.

'Have you ever had any dealings with Indians?'

'Like in the movies? Redskins?'

'Never mind,' said Montalbano. And he said goodbye to the miraculous cook, giving him a hug.

*

In the five days he'd been away – as Fazio reported to him – nothing of any importance had happened. Carmelo Arnone, the man with the tobacco shop near the train station, had fired four shots at Angelo Cannizzaro, haberdasher, over a woman. Mimì Augello, who happened to be in the area, had courageously confronted the gunman and disarmed him.

'So,' Montalbano commented, 'Cannizzaro came away with little more than a good scare.'

It was well known to everyone in town that Carmelo Arnone didn't know how to handle a gun and couldn't even hit a cow at point-blank range.

'Well, no.'

'He hit him?' asked Montalbano, stunned.

Actually, Fazio went on to explain, he hadn't hit his target this time either. One of the bullets, though, after striking a lamp post, had ricocheted back and ended up between Cannizzaro's shoulder blades. The wound was nothing, the bullet had lost all its force by then. But in no time the rumour had spread all over town that the cowardly Carmelo Arnone had shot Angelo Cannizzaro in the back. So Cannizzaro's brother, Pasqualino, who dealt in broad beans and wore glasses with lenses an inch thick, armed himself, tracked down Carmelo Arnone, and shot at him, missing twice. That is, he missed both the target and the identity of the target. Deceived by a strong family resemblance, he had mistaken Carmelo's brother Filippo, who owned a fruit and vegetable store, for Carmelo himself. As for missing the target, the first shot had ended up God knows where, while the second had injured the little finger on the left hand of a shopkeeper from Canicattì who'd come to Vigàta on business. At this point the pistol had jammed, otherwise Pasqualino Cannizzarì, firing blindly, would surely have wrought another slaughter of the innocents.

Ah and also, there were two robberies, four bag snatchings and three cars torched. Routine stuff.

There was a knock at the door and Tortorella came in after pushing the door open with his foot, arms laden with a good six or seven pounds of papers.

'Shall we make good use of your time while you're here?'

'Tortorè, you make it sound like I've been away for a hundred years!'

Since he never signed anything without first carefully reading what it was about, Montalbano had barely dispatched a couple of pounds of documents when it was already lunchtime. Though he felt some stirring in the pit of his stomach, he decided not to go to the Trattoria San Calogero. He wasn't ready yet to desecrate the memory of Tanino, the cook directly inspired by the Madonna. The betrayal, when it came, would have to be justified, at least in part, by abstinence.

He finished signing papers at eight that evening, with aches not only in his fingers, but in his whole arm.

*

By the time he got home, he was ravenous; in the pit of his stomach there now was a hole. How should he proceed? Should he open the oven and fridge and see what Adelina had made for him? He reasoned that, if going from one restaurant to another could technically be called a betrayal, to go from Tanino to Adelina certainly could not. Rather, it might be better defined as a return to the family fold after an adulterous interlude. The oven was empty. In the fridge he found ten or so olives, three sardines and a bit of Lampedusan tuna in a small glass jar. On the kitchen table there was some bread wrapped in paper, next to a note from the housekeeper.

> Since you didna tell me when you was commin back, I cook and cook and then I gotta thro alla this good food away. I'm not gonna cook no more.

She didn't want to go on wasting things, clearly, but more importantly, she must have felt offended because he hadn't told her where he was going ('All right, so Ima just a maid, sir, but sommatime you treeta me jes like a maid!').

He listlessly ate a couple of olives with bread, which he decided to accompany with some of his father's wine. He turned the television on to the Free Channel. It was time for the news.

Nicolò Zito was finishing up a commentary on the arrest of a town council man in Fela for embezzlement and graft. Then he moved on to the latest stories. On the outskirts of Sommatina, between Caltanissetta and Enna, a woman's body had been recovered in an advanced state of decomposition.

Montalbano sat bolt upright in his armchair.

The woman had been strangled, stuffed into a bag and thrown into a rather deep, dry well. Beside her they found a small suitcase that led to the victim's identification. Karima Moussa, aged thirty-four, a native of Tunis who had moved to Vigàta a few years earlier.

The photo of Karima and François that the inspector had given Nicolò appeared on the screen.

Did the viewing audience remember the Free Channel's report on the woman's disappearance? No trace, meanwhile, had turned up of the little boy, her son. According to Inspector Diliberto, who was conducting the investigation, the killer might have been the Tunisian woman's unknown procurer. There nevertheless remained, in the inspector's opinion, numerous details to be cleared up.

Montalbano whinnied, turned off the TV, and smiled. Lohengrin Pera had kept his word. He stood up, stretched, sat back down and immediately fell asleep in the armchair. An animal slumber, probably dreamless, like a sack of potatoes.

✶

The next morning, from his office, he called the commissioner and invited himself to dinner. Then he called police headquarters in Sommatino.

'Diliberto? Montalbano here. I'm calling from Vigàta.'

'Hello, colleague. What can I do for you?'

'I wanted to know about that woman you found in the well.'

'Karima Moussa.'

'Yes. Are you absolutely certain about the identification?'

'Without a shadow of a doubt. In her bag, among other things, we found an ATM card from the Banca Agricola di Montelusa.'

'Excuse me for interrupting, but anyone, you see, could have put—'

'Let me finish. Three years ago, this woman had an accident for which she was given twelve stitches in her right arm at Montelusa Hospital. It checks out. The scar was still visible despite the body's advanced state of decomposition.'

'Listen, Diliberto, I just got back to Vigàta this morning after a few days off. I'm short on news and found out about the body on a local TV station. They reported you still had some questions.'

'Not about the identification. But I'm certain the woman was killed and buried somewhere else, not where we found her after receiving an anonymous tip. So my question is: why did they dig her up and move the body? What need was there to do that?'

'What makes you so sure they did?'

'You see, Karima's suitcase was soiled with bodily waste from its first period alongside the corpse. And in order to carry the suitcase to the well where it was found, they wrapped it in newspaper.'

'So?'

'The newspaper was only three days old. Whereas the woman had been killed at least ten days earlier. The coroner would bet his life on it. So I need to work out why she was moved. And I have no idea; I just can't understand it.'

Montalbano had an idea, but he couldn't tell his colleague what it was. If only those fuckheads in the secret services could do something right for once! Like the time when, wanting to make people believe that a certain Libyan aeroplane had crashed in Sila on a specific day, they staged a show of explosions and flames, and then, in the autopsy, it was determined that the pilot had actually died fifteen days earlier from the impact. The flying cadaver.

*

After a simple but elegant dinner, Montalbano and his superior retired to the study. The commissioner's wife withdrew in turn to watch television.

Montalbano's story was long and so detailed that he

didn't even leave out his voluntary crushing of Lohengrin Pera's little gold eyeglasses. At a certain point, the report turned into a confession. But the commissioner's absolution was slow in coming. He was truly annoyed at having been left out of the game.

'I'm angry with you, Montalbano. You denied me a chance to amuse myself a little before calling it quits.'

*

My dear Livia,

This letter will surprise you for at least two reasons. The first is the letter itself, my having written it and sent it. Unwritten letters I've sent you by the bushel, at least one a day. I realized that in all these years, I've only sent you an occasional miserly postcard with a few 'bureaucratic, inspectorly' greetings, as you called them.

The second reason, which will delight you as much as surprise you, is its content.

Since you left exactly fifty-five days ago (as you can see, I keep track), many things have happened, some of which concern us directly. To say they 'happened', however, is incorrect; it would be more accurate to write that I made them happen.

You reproached me once for a certain tendency I have to play God by altering the course of events (for others) through omissions great and small, and even through more or less damnable falsifications. Maybe it's true. Actually, it most certainly is. But don't you think this, too, is part of my job?

Whatever the case, you should know at once that I'm about to tell you of another supposed transgression of mine, one that was aimed, however, at turning a chain of events in our favour, and was therefore not for or against anyone else. But first I want to tell you about François.

Neither you nor I have even mentioned his name since the last night you spent in Marinella, when you reproached me for not having realized that the boy could become the son we would never have. What's more, you were hurt by the way I had the child taken from you. But, you see, I was terrified, and with good reason. He had become a dangerous witness, and I was afraid they would make him disappear (or 'neutralize' him, as they say euphemistically).

The omission of that name has weighed heavily on our phone conversations, making them evasive and a little loveless. Today I want to make it clear to you that if I never once mentioned François before now, it was to keep you from nurturing dangerous illusions. And if I'm writing to you about him now, it is because this fear has subsided.

Do you remember that morning in Marinella when François ran away to look for his mother? Well, as I was walking him home, he told me he didn't want to end up in an orphanage. And I replied that this would never happen. I gave him my word of honour, and we shook on it. I made a promise, and I will keep it at all costs.

In these fifty-five days Mimì Augello, at my request, has been phoning his sister three times a week to see how the boy is doing. The answers have always been reassuring.

The day before yesterday, in Mimì's company, I went to see him (by the way, you ought to write Mimì a letter thanking him for his generosity and friendship). I had a chance to observe François for a few minutes while he was playing with Mimì's nephew, who's the same age. He was cheerful and carefree. As soon as he saw me (he recognized me at once), his expression changed. He sort of turned sad. Children's memories, like those of the elderly, are intermittent. I'm sure the thought of his mother had come back to him. He gave me a big hug and then, looking at me with bright, tearless eyes — he doesn't seem to me a boy who cries easily — he didn't ask me what I was afraid he'd ask, that is, if I had any news of Karima. In a soft voice, he said only, 'Take me to Livia.'

Not to his mother. To you. He must be convinced he'll never see his mother again. And unfortunately, he's right.

You know that from the very first, based on unhappy experience, I was convinced that Karima had been murdered. To do what I had in mind, I had to make a dangerous move that would bring the accomplices to her murder out in the open. The next step was to force them to produce the woman's body in such a way that, when it was found, it would be certain to be identified. It all went well. And so I was able to act 'officially' on behalf of François, who has now been declared motherless. The commissioner was a tremendous help to me, putting all his many acquaintances to work. If Karima's body had not been found, my steps would have surely been hindered by endless bureaucratic red tape, which would have delayed the resolution of our problem for years and years.

I realize this letter is getting too long, so I'll change register.

1) In the eyes of the law, Italian as well as Tunisian, François is in a paradoxical situation. In fact, he's an orphan who doesn't exist, inasmuch as his birth was never registered either in Sicily or Tunisia.

2) The judge in Montelusa who deals with these questions has sort of straightened out his status, but only for as long as it takes to go through the necessary procedures. He has assigned him temporarily to the care of Mimì's sister.

3) The same judge has informed me that while it is theoretically possible in Italy for an unmarried woman to adopt a child, in reality it's all talk. And he cited the case of an actress who was subjected to years of judicial pronouncements, opinions and decisions, each one contradicting the last.

4) The best way to expedite matters, in the judge's opinion, is for us to get married.

5) So get your papers ready.

A hug and a kiss. Salvo

P.S. A friend of mine in Vigàta who's a notary will administer a fund *of one-half billion lire in François's name, which he'll be free to use when he comes legally of age. I find it fitting that our son should be officially born the exact moment he sets foot in our house, and more than fitting that he should be helped through life by his real mother, whose money that was.*

❧

YOUR FATHER IS NEARING THE END DO NOT DELAY IF YOU EVER WANT TO SEE HIM AGAIN. ARCANGELO PRESTIFILIPPO.

He'd been expecting these words, but when he read them the dull ache returned, as when he'd first found out. Except that now it was compounded by the anguish of knowing what duty required him to do: to bend down over the bed, kiss his father's forehead, feel his dry, dying breath, look him in the eye, say a few comforting words. Would he have the strength? Drenched in sweat, he thought this must be the inevitable test, if indeed it was true that he must grow up, as Professor Pintacuda had said.

I will teach François not to fear my death, he thought. And from this thought, which surprised him by the very fact that he'd had it, he derived a temporary peace of mind.

❧

Right outside the gates of Valmontana, after four straight hours of driving, was a road sign indicating the route to follow for the Clinica Porticelli.

He left the car in the well-ordered car park and went in. He felt his heart beating right under his Adam's apple.

'My name is Montalbano. I'd like to see my father who's staying here.'

The person behind the desk eyed him for a moment, then pointed to a small waiting room.

'Please make yourself comfortable. I'll call Dr Brancato for you.'

He sat down in an armchair and picked up one of the magazines that lay on a small table. He put it back down at once. His hands were so sweaty they had wet the cover.

The doctor, a very serious-looking man of about fifty in a white smock, came in and held out his hand to him.

'Mr Montalbano? I am very, very sorry to have to tell you that your father died peacefully two hours ago.'

'Thank you,' said Montalbano.

The doctor looked at him, slightly bewildered. But it wasn't him the inspector was thanking.

Author's Note

One critic, when reviewing my book *The Terracotta Dog*, wrote that Vigàta, the non-existent town in which all my novels are set, is 'the most invented city of the most typical Sicily.'

I cite these words in support of the requisite declaration that all names, places and situations in this book have been *invented* out of whole cloth. Even the number plate.

If fantasy has somehow coincided with reality, the blame, in my opinion, lies with reality.

The novel is dedicated to Flem. He liked stories like this.

Notes

page 3 – **sardines a beccafico** – *Sarde a beccafico* are a famous Sicilian speciality named after a small bird, the *beccafico* (*Sylvia borin*, garden warbler in English), which is particularly fond of figs; indeed the name *beccafico* means 'fig-pecker'. The headless, cleaned sardines are stuffed with sautéed breadcrumbs, pine nuts, raisins and anchovies, then rolled up in such a way that, when removed from the oven, they resemble the bird.

page 8 – **'the prefect'** – The *prefetto* is the local representative of the central Italian government; one is assigned to each province. They are part of the national, not local bureaucracy.

page 31 – **alalonga all'agrodolce** – *Alalonga* (literally 'longwing') is a particularly delicious species of small tuna. *All'agrodolce* means 'sweet and sour', and in this case involves sautéing a small steak of the fish in a sauce of vinegar, oil, sugar and parsley.

page 31 – **The Northern League . . . towards secession** – The Lega Nord is a right-wing political party based in the northern regions of Italy (Lombardy, Veneto, Piedmont) and known for its prejudices against foreign immigrants and southern Italians. Until recently they had been threatening to constitute a separate national entity under the historically dubious name of Padania (after the Po River, which runs from the Piedmont through Lombardy and the Veneto), and to secede from the Italian republic.

page 40 – **They spread their hands apart, looking sorrowful** – Spreading the hands apart, palms open, is a gesture typical of southern Italians and seen often among Italian Americans, most notably Al Pacino in many of his movie roles. It usually expresses helplessness and resignation to fate.

page 42 – **A smell of stale perfume, burnt straw in colour** – As seen in the first two novels, Montalbano synaesthetically associates colours with smells.

page 54 – ***E te lo vojo dì / che sò stato io*** – 'And I want to say / that it was me.' The lines are a refrain from a popular Italian song of the early 1970s by the Fratelli DeAngelis. In it a man confesses to a friend that it was he who committed an unsolved crime of passion some thirty years before, and that he has kept the truth inside him all these years.

page 54 – **'goat-tied'** – The Sicilian word is *incaprettato* (containing the word for goat, *capra*), and it refers to a particularly cruel method of execution used by the Mafia, where the victim, face down, has a rope looped around his neck and then tied to his feet, which are raised behind his back, as in hog-tying. Fatigue eventually forces him to lower his feet, strangling himself in the process.

page 73 – **'Italy is a Republic founded on construction work'** – A send-up of the first sentence of the Italian constitution: 'Italy is a Republic founded on work.'

page 77 – **a gesture that meant 'gone away'** – Normally this consists of tapping the edge of the right hand against the open left palm, a sign used equally in Italy, France, Spain and North Africa to mean 'let's go' or 'gone'.

page 83 – **Montalbano brought his fingertips together, pointing upwards, artichoke-like** – This is a familiar gesture of questioning used by all Italians.

page 109 – **he was going out to the nearest tobacco shop** – Tobacco products in Italy are distributed by the state monopoly and sold only in licensed shops, bars and cafes.

page 111 – **when Montelusa was called Kerkent** – The fictional Montelusa is modelled on the city of Agrigento (the ancient Agrigentum), called Girgenti by the Sicilians and Kerkent by the Arabs.

page 113 – **children's late-morning snacks** – Lunch in Italy isn't usually eaten until one or one-thirty in the afternoon, and mothers often pack a snack for their children to quell their late-morning hunger.

page 125 – *torroncini* – Marzipan pastries filled with pumpkin jam and covered with roasted almonds.

page 127 – **'the Lacapra case'** – Lapécora means 'the sheep', while Lacapra means 'the goat'.

page 128 – **pasta 'ncasciata** – A casserole of *pasta corta* (that is, elbow macaroni, penne, ziti, mezzi ziti, or something similar), tomato sauce, ground beef, Parmesan and béchamel.

page 135 – **'By repenting . . . turning state's witness against the Mafia'** – In Italy, Mafia turncoats are called *pentiti*, 'repenters', and many people, like Montalbano, believe they are treated too leniently by the government.

page 135 – *càlia e simenza* – A snack food of chickpeas and pumpkin seeds, sometimes with peanuts as well.

page 160 – **'Pippo Baudo'** – A famous Italian television personality and master of ceremonies for a number of different variety shows.

page 163 – **No one must ever know that Inspector Montalbano was rescued by the carabinieri** – The carabinieri, considered not very intelligent in the popular imagination, are a national paramilitary police force. They and the local police forces are often in competition with each other.

page 166 – **'On Saturday'** – Italian children attend school from Monday to Saturday.

pages 183–4 – **Didìo . . . 'The Wrath of God'** – *Di Dio* means 'of God' in Italian.

page 195 – **Totò and Peppino** – Totò, born Antonio de Curtis to a princely family, was one of the greatest comic actors of twentieth-century Italy. He made many famous films with Peppino, born Peppino De Filippo, another great comic and, like Totò, from Naples.

page 196 – **Wasn't that title abolished half a century ago?** – Much used and abused during the Fascist era, the title 'Your Excellency' was finally banned after the Second World War, though many government dignitaries still defy the ban.

page 229 – **'Guarda come dondolo . . . col twist'** – 'See how I sway, see how I sway, doing the twist.' Lines from a popular song written and performed by Edoardo Vianello.

page 244 – **'Montanelli'** – Indro Montanelli (1909–2001) was a famous journalist who began his long career during the time of the Fascists, whom he initially supported. He continued to work as a columnist and social critic until his death.

page 248 – **to compensate . . . for his . . . surname** – *Pera* means 'pear' in Italian.

NOTES

page 267 – **'Celeste Aida'** – A famous aria from Giuseppe Verdi's opera *Aida*.

page 273 – **'the miracle of the blood of San Gennaro'** – San Gennaro (St Januarius) is the patron saint of Naples. Though little is known about him, his celebrity lies in the alleged miracle of the 'liquefaction' of his blood, which is kept in a small glass vial in the eponymous cathedral of that city. The miracle is believed to occur some eighteen times a year, but the main event is on 19 September, the saint's feast day, when large crowds always gather to witness it. Failure to liquefy is believed to be a dire portent.

page 287 – **a certain Libyan aeroplane . . . from the impact** – On 27 June 1980, an Italian airliner crashed into the sea near the Sicilian island of Ustica. All eighty-one people on board died, and the incident has remained shrouded in mystery. The most prevalent theory is that the plane was shot down by a missile during a NATO exercise, but NATO has always denied this. The radar data, meanwhile, has disappeared. Many rumours (never confirmed) have since surfaced saying that an aerial battle had taken place during an attempt by NATO to shoot down the plane in which Colonel Ghaddafi was travelling. Whatever the case, shortly after the incident a fallen Libyan war plane was recovered in the Calabrian mountains, which the Italian secret service said had crashed the same day as the airliner. The only problem was that the pilot would have to have been dead while flying the aeroplane, since a verifiable autopsy (after an earlier one had been proven false) showed that he'd died twelve days before the crash.

Notes compiled by Stephen Sartarelli